I0815391

A YEAR OF GARDEN-INSPIRED LIVING

Quarto.com

First Published in 2025 by Cool Springs Press, an imprint of The Quarto Group,
100 Cummings Center, Suite 265-D, Beverly, MA 01915, USA.
T (978) 282-9590 F (978) 283-2742

EEA Representation, WTS Tax d.o.o.,
Žanova ulica 3, 4000 Kranj, Slovenia.
www.wts-tax.si

Cool Springs Press titles are also available at discount for retail, wholesale, promotional, and bulk purchase. For details, contact the Special Sales Manager by email at specialsales@quarto.com or by mail at The Quarto Group, Attn: Special Sales Manager, 100 Cummings Center, Suite 265-D, Beverly, MA 01915, USA.

29 28 27 26 25 1 2 3 4 5

ISBN: 978-0-7603-9515-8

Digital edition published in 2025
eISBN: 978-0-7603-9516-5

Library of Congress Cataloging-in-Publication Data is available.

Design and page layout: Cindy Samargia Laun
Illustration: Briana Kranz | www.brianakranz.com
Front cover illustration: Sodel Vladyslav / Adobe Stock
and DAIYAN MD TALHA / Adobe Stock

Printed in Guangdong,China TT 062025

A YEAR OF GARDEN-INSPIRED LIVING

season by season

LINDA VATER
author of *The Elegant and Edible Garden*

Illustration by Briana Kranz

COOL SPRINGS PRESS

CONTENTS

INTRODUCTION

"What do you know for sure?" It's a probing question I like to ask people I want to get to know better, more intimately, and on a deeper level. Once we have gotten beyond the superficial topics of weather, geography, family, and gardening, of course. I find the responses and ensuing follow-up conversation to this question fascinating, insightful, and revelatory for all.

Assuming, that is, that the person being questioned has an answer.

I've noticed that the older the person being questioned, the more likely there is to be a ready response. This is not always true (I know quite a few young people who can answer the question just as readily), but in my experience, very reflective and self-aware "old souls" tend to greatly ruminate on the topic and find it an intellectual exercise well worth the challenge.

It is a question we can ask ourselves in a quest for wisdom, understanding, life enrichment, and clarity. Our answers may be few, but ah—how instructive they are! They serve as a lens through which we can look at life and our day-to-day moments and relationships.

So, what do I know for sure—at my age, at this specific moment in time, and at this stage in my life? It is a short list; I have come up with only three answers with certitude and a degree of confidence as to their truth. Here is my short list:

> *The only thing that is constant is change.* We all intuitively and empirically know it to be true.
>
> *A person's (and sometimes even a garden's) greatest strength is its greatest weakness.* And finally . . .
>
> *It's the everyday, small things in life that are **truly** important.* Small gestures of kindness, small expressions of beauty and our common humanity, and small but consistent habits and behaviors made over a long period of time can add up to something significant; something that makes a difference; something that helps you hold your head up when things are feeling low. Possibly even the holy grail we all chase: contentment and joy in our daily lives. And to live happily ever after, one moment at a time.

A spectacular arbor consumed by roses in spring is undeniably magnificent. I know from experience. With lots of training, pruning, nurturing, and sweat equity over time, such magnificence can be brought to bear, however short-lived the bloom. Until, of course, a deadly virus or storm strikes it down. But the scent of one unexpected bloom, placed strategically on a bedside table? Such a thing can keep me in comfortable, charming company when I lie reading in bed, too anxious to sleep. When I wake in the middle of the night with a severe case of imaginary "horribles," it has the power to console and reassure me that beauty exists still, eventually lulling me back to my dreams. It's just one example of a small and humble thing having oversized influence and consequence—one small note playing at just the right time.

My goal in this book is to capture some of the small but important moments of beauty, fun, thoughtfulness, charm, and creative imagination that make a life—especially a garden-inspired life—worth living. Activities, gestures, and practices that soften and improve the quality of our days and the quality of our relationships. Give some of these ideas a try. See what a difference small moments can make in **your** days, in **your** life . . . and the lives of those around you.

Linda

Why Not Try . . .

EXPERIENCING THE SEASONS
purposely, consciously, lovingly,
and stylishly?

WINTERING

nesting,
hibernating,
whispering,
cocooning,
flickering,
hungering

Of all the seasons, winter is the most elemental, don't you agree? Raw and cold and pure, sometimes stark. Devoid of color and leafiness, pattern endures—skeletal tree branches silhouetted against crystal blue sky, pixelated seed heads for birds to consume, and melting ice and frost along the gables and shingles of rooftops. The concentric circles formed by wooden spoons stirring roux in a Dutch oven prepare a blank canvas awaiting yet more patterns, this time patterns of flavor and texture to create a sauce, a stew, or a soup. We pile our blankets high, reveling in the wooly deliciousness of plaid stacked on plaid stacked on plaid—all in grids of a chosen color, chosen hue, and chosen texture. We create still-lives for our homes out of whatever we find intrinsically beautiful in our basements, gardens, and attics. This fuels our creativity and keeps unnecessary consumption to a minimum. It may be cold outside, but inside we are fired up with a desire to conjure comfort and calm in our daily rounds.

Happily, the slow pace of these first months of the year gives us the time to search out or create such moody pleasures. Not unlike the landscape outdoors, our homes and lives are more quiet, more contemplative, purer, and renewed by a new year—they are fresh blank canvases to paint on colorful possibilities. We grow attentive to our own life patterns, the good and the bad of them. Getting up early in the quiet of a dark morning, we can plan the day, plan the meals, make the list of what it takes for something to happen. No worthy endeavor too small or inconsequential to escape our forethought and intention. Maybe new patterns are formed and old patterns relinquished or modified? Oh, the prospects! What if, we think. What if?

Keepsakes Contained

It was one of the most intriguing gifts she had ever seen: three small clay bowls containing mementos and small tokens of history from the giver's home in the Blue Ridge Mountains. One contained three bullets—buck and ball ammunition dating back to the Civil War, found in the foothills nearby. Another was filled with beautiful small pebbles from a stream in the same area. The third held tiny immature pinecones—as if collected by a fairy. All three bowls were nestled in a bed of straw within a small rectangular crate. Given that the recipient was a Civil War scholar, she knew it would be **very** warmly received. What an ever-so-clever idea, she thought, that could be executed in any number of ways. It delighted her to no end. The power of three. Three tiny bowls, to be exact.

Wee Collections

WHY NOT TRY collecting small bowls that speak to your personal aesthetic, be they ceramic, wood, marble, porcelain, or even woven? Your collecting muse might be a certain color, pattern, texture, or finish. Use them to collect foraged treasures like acorns or shells; to contain your daily ration of vitamins or meds; or as individual salt and pepper cellars at your dining table. Typically inexpensive, these little treasures can be found at thrift stores or garage sales.

Baking Up a Storm

Bonnie had never stored her baking canisters anywhere but in the pantry, on her kitchen counters, or on a baking cart in the corner next to her refrigerator when space was tight. But it never occurred to her to have a baking **drawer** . . . one located right underneath the section of countertop that held her heavy stand mixer and mixing bowls. Now, this might seem a small detail in the scheme of things, but to Bonnie it was life changing—or at least baking life-changing, because it was all so much easier. A friend of hers had done the same, and waxed episodic about its merits and convenience. So into the drawer—a deep drawer, mind you—Bonnie put her canisters of flour, sugar, brown sugar, baking soda, baking powder, and measuring cups. She didn't even need to lift them out of their housing. She could just dip, spoon, and measure the ingredients right into the bowl of her mixer. From drawer to mixing bowl with hardly any movement at all. It almost seemed too good to be true. Her family thought the same. They had never seen so many batches of homemade cookies and banana bread.

Open and Shut Baking

WHY NOT TRY organizing a baking drawer or cart devoted to all things baking? Include common baking ingredients and keep measuring cups and spoons in easy reach.

A Delightful Treat

They always loved visiting the Wyler home. Everything seemed so personalized and intentional, unique to them and the atmosphere they created in their home—even if you dropped by unexpectedly. In the cold winter months, you could always count on them for a cup of their special tea blend—Mrs. Wyler purchased it from a coffee and tea shop nearby. In fact, she had a couple of "house tea blends" that she served, depending on the season. The Wylers did the same with wine—at the beginning of each season they would carefully taste-test several varieties selected by their favorite neighborhood vintner, and based on its deliciousness and its price point, would choose one and buy a case or two as their own "house wine" for that time of year.

These kinds of gracious notes always made the notion of going to the Wyler house such a delightful treat. Warm, inviting, thoughtful—no wonder guests always felt so comfortable and welcome there.

House Favorites

WHY NOT TRY declaring a house tea, wine, or a playlist for the season? Invite others for a taste test party to weigh in on your selections. Have small bites to eat as palate cleansers in between varieties.

Great Grommets!

After years of stressing over what type of festive outdoor lights to put up for the holidays (and one year paying **far** too much to have a company do it for her), Missy decided it was time to take control and come up with a classy and easy decor formula she could use from year to year. She found exactly what she was looking for in the pages of a 1950s *House Beautiful* magazine: a charming scene, snow-covered of course, with four traditional and identical lighted wreathes hanging in each of the four front windows. What captured her attention especially was the way the evergreen wreathes were suspended and hanging elegantly—about 12 inches (31 cm) from the top of the window frame. The instructions were clear and simple: Loop a sturdy wide stretch of ribbon through the top of the wreath frame, but before doing so, install two circular metal grommets on both ends. She knew her local shoe repair shop could do it for her. Then, using these handy holes, hang and suspend the ribbons from a nail that was inconspicuous enough to remain in place year-round. Craft matching bows of the same ribbon, and voila! A classy and easy installation each holiday season. Using realistic-looking faux wreathes would make the job even easier and less costly, Missy realized. Stress free, easy, elegant, and in her favorite holiday motif—the wreath.

Holiday Decor Made Easy

WHY NOT TRY using grommets in lengths of wide ribbon to make hanging your holiday wreaths a breeze?

Holiday Explosion

Her friend Bessel brought her a basket of them. Velvety, suedelike, sage-green pods from the massive wisteria vine growing up an equally massive iron trellis on the back of his home. He knew she loved such things, especially in that unique green color she adored. And indeed, she did love them. She used them in her centerpiece for Thanksgiving and also in a floral arrangement on her mantle. As he suspected, she had great fun with them, using them as decorative accents in multiple spaces throughout her home. And to her great and unexpected surprise, one evening gentle popping noises continued rhythmically and repetitively throughout the night. A late-night inspection turned up nothing. Fire, mice, and expired canned goods were all ruled out. But the next morning, while having coffee in the parlor, the evidence of the previous night's disturbances were everywhere. **Every one** of the wisteria pods, as if on schedule, had exploded—their dark button-shaped seeds escaping the velvety casings and scattering everywhere. And in the birthing process, the casings had twisted and contorted themselves into the most symmetrical spiral shapes imaginable, equally as beautiful after giving birth as before. In fact, she thought, they would look so pretty as natural ornaments suspended from a Christmas tree. She raced to the phone to call Bessel and disclose what her detective work had uncovered.

Explosive Fall Decor

WHY NOT TRY using velvety wisteria seed pods as fall decor, or even as ornaments to hang on a tree?

The Hanging of the Greens

Holly stood in the office break room, coffee in hand, ready to set the scene for the annual holiday party. She pulled out a long piece of artificial greenery from a red tub and gave it a good fluffing. Next, she grabbed the shower tension rod she'd bought earlier that morning on her way to work. She recruited a coworker who helped her place it securely in the door frame leading into the break room, looping the garland around it, twinkle lights and all.

With appreciative laughter and applause at her cleverness from coworkers nearby, Holly plugged in the lights, illuminating the doorway and all who passed through it. A bit of color from some ornaments glamorized it even more and tassels of large sugar pinecones completed the look. "But no mistletoe," her boss, Joan, chuckled. "This is a workspace, after all."

Festive Doorway

WHY NOT TRY using inexpensive tension rods to hang greenery at Christmas? No nails or hammer required. Just a stepping stool . . . or a tall elf.

Holiday Honey

Charlotte was finding the holidays, well, inconvenient this year. An unusually strong case of "too much to do and too little time" had hit her big time. She usually took great pleasure in shopping for gifts close to home. Shopping local yielded very personal gifts unique to the recipient's personality and interests. But limited time was dictating her holiday shopping this year, and she needed it to be quick and easy. She was pondering all of this while sipping her afternoon tea with honey. Delicious honey. Decadent honey. Like liquid caramel honey. It was manuka honey—a gift from her daughter-in-law who introduced her to its incomparable flavor and healthy profile. Then it struck her—it was the perfect gift for everyone on her list! As an added bonus, it came attractively boxed with a cute little wooden spoon and would be easy and fun to wrap. **Done!** She thought smugly after buying multiple jars to gift for the coming holidays, *No regifting this liquid gold!* Everyone on her list would love it.

Good Gift Idea on Repeat

WHY NOT TRY pressing the easy button at holiday gift giving time by selecting a single gift that's cheaper and easier by the dozen? Pick one item everyone is sure to love.

A Basket of Comfort

Jini and Jane didn't know her well, but when they heard that a neighbor down the street had suffered the unexpected and tragic loss of a sibling, they wanted to acknowledge it in some way. Something more than just a sympathy card. A basket of comforts seemed appropriate. They proceeded to fill a wicker basket with things they themselves found comforting. Teabags, dark chocolate, homemade chicken soup, and a couple of books to read. Since it was winter, some warm, fuzzy socks and a scented candle with matches completed the gift. Given the magnitude of the sorrow, they knew it wasn't much; still, it was something. And they knew from experience that gestures of kindness and sympathy from unexpected places were a comfort in and of themselves.

Filled with Comfort, Care, and Concern

WHY NOT TRY composing a basket of comforts for someone who is hurting? Just ask yourself what would be of comfort to you and you have the contents of a thoughtful gift for someone sad or in pain.

An Atypical Color Palette for the Holidays

Until they moved to the Cottage on the Hill, she had no interest in using anything other than the most traditional of colors for Christmas: red and deep green, maybe some white, silver, or gold . . . and plaid, of course, in the same hues. But this year . . . **this** year . . . she wanted to step out of her comfort zone. The bright southern sun cascading through the diamond pane windows painted woodwork and walls, and the overall brightness of the spaces called for something less intense, less saturated, less heavy. More celestial than earthy. She was going to embrace the colors of a winter wonderland instead of the colors of a Victorian Christmas: sky blue, pale blue, and linen blue, with white, cream, and pale silver. It brought to mind snow and steel-blue winter-gray skies. The more muted, less traditional palette would seem fresh and less tied to the past. Not that that was a bad thing, it was just that she was ready for a new start, new hues, and a new way of expressing herself during the holidays. A clean holiday palette, cool and ethereal. A "lightness of being" palette. *Yes,* she thought to herself, *that was it.* She wanted a "lightness of being" Christmas this year. Elegant, crystalline, and wonderful.

Holiday Shakeup

WHY NOT TRY using a nontraditional holiday color palette for Thanksgiving, Christmas, Hanukkah, or Kwanzaa? Shake it up a bit.

Childhood Reflected in a Marble

Margaret walked through the aisles of the small town's five and dime store. The planked floors squeaked, and with each squeaky footstep the scent of 100-year-old wood and youthful memories filled the air. It was just as she remembered it from her childhood visits to her grandparents' home in their small German town—where a trip to this very store was the highlight. Miraculously, the aisles were still filled with childish delights: locally made taffy and fudge; candy necklaces; coin-operated machines that, with the twist of a knob, spit out jawbreakers or plastic orbs with tiny treasures stuffed inside; muslin bags filled with ball and jacks sets and tiny tubes of candy lipstick. But when she saw the mesh bags filled with colorful marbles, like small glass planets, she went weak in the knees. Happy memories came flooding back. She swooped up two bundles with almost as much delight as she had many years ago. When she returned home, even before unpacking one piece of clothing, she dug out the small sacks of the marbles, cut them open, and delighted at the sound they made tumbling into the blue

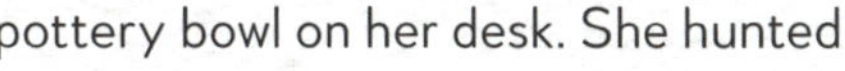

pottery bowl on her desk. She hunted down her favorite pens and pencils and took great pleasure in nestling them into the marble mounds. She looked forward to sitting at her desk in the morning with the east sun shining through the windows, making rainbows and sparkles on her bowl of colorful, translucent memories.

Marble Makeover

WHY NOT TRY filling a bowl with colorful marbles and placing it on your desk to hold pencils, pens, and other daily necessities?

Have You Heard of "Jolabokaflod"?

Jolabokaflod in Iceland is a delightful holiday tradition. During WWII, paper was one of the few nonrationed items in Iceland, so Icelanders exchanged books as gifts. Traditionally, the books are given on Christmas Eve, and then everyone gathers to spend the night reading. Noel **loved** the idea of reading together almost as much as she loved books. Ever since she learned to read, maybe even earlier, Noel felt most safe, secure, and happy when she and her parents and brother would read together in front of the fireplace. Together, but in completely different worlds, depending on the book in hand and where it transported each of them. Her dad would make them all hot chocolate, ensuring each person had the same number of marshmallows to keep the peace (sometimes there was even a bonus candy cane), and then within the comfort of their own respective book nooks, they would get serious about the matter at hand: Reading. Sometimes there were soft Christmas carols in the background, sometimes just the sound of the crackling fire. When she learned of Jolabokaflod, she was thrilled to be able to put a name to the practice. Jolabokaflod in one's own *bokahorn*, or book nook . . . another Icelandic term she had grown to love as well.

All Together Now

WHY NOT TRY creating a book nook for cozy reading either alone or with others? Keep a warm throw (maybe even a heated one) nearby. Candles and warm beverages set the mood and entice one and all to read more.

Solving a Problem

It was an old house, after all, Constance thought to herself. At almost 100 years old, it could be forgiven for its lack of electrical outlets and other twenty-first-century conveniences. Still, it would be so lovely to be able to put sconces and lamps in areas that had no outlets nearby but cried out for some illumination. Not only would light be provided but also the jewel-like quality of the brass and other metallics would perfectly complete certain spaces in her home. While flipping through a magazine, Constance read an article about another homeowner who had solved just such a problem through the use of ingenious battery-powered lighting, requiring no hard wiring, requisite holes in walls, or the expenses associated with getting power to those locations. Apparently, all sorts of different rechargeable lightbulbs, lamps, sconces, and even candles were available for locations where electricity is not an option.

She immediately searched online for battery-powered brass sconces to flank a major work of art in her dining room, as well as brass and black lamps for a number of different areas. She even created a discreet area where they could all be regularly charged and repowered. Oh, how far we had come in the last 100 years, Constance thought to herself. Another old home problem solved with an ingenious solution.

Look! No Cords!

WHY NOT TRY using a rechargeable battery lamp when an outlet isn't available? Table lamps, sconces, and task lighting are all available.

Stand It on Its Head

It had been sitting in the back of her garage for the longest time. A galvanized iron table base with four flared legs and a round circular hollow top, upon which a thick piece of glass once rested. A handy, good-looking table until the move, when the glass top got chipped. But she liked the industrial handsomeness of the metal base and felt sure she could use it in some unique way in the future. Then inspiration struck. She had been gifted a beautiful concrete saucer bird bath from an appreciative client and wanted to give it the placement and stature in her garden it deserved. It would look lovely just nestled in her garden bed, but Jill wanted its beauty to be more prominent . . . and that required elevating it in some way. In an aha! moment, Jill thought of the iron stand tucked away in the garage. Sure enough, if she turned the table base upside down, the four flared legs would perfectly support the concrete saucer at just the right height. The scale and heft of the iron was the perfect material to enhance the concrete. When she placed it in her garden underneath a large redbud tree—and just within sight when looking out her kitchen window—she knew it was perfect.

First One Way, Then Another

WHY NOT TRY turning a piece of furniture upside down—especially stands, stools, and small tables—for a novel new use? Be resourceful and inventive with what you already own.

Sea Sickness and Hot Beverages

It turned out to be a disaster of a trip. Despite the beautiful renovation of the small vessel, including gorgeous teak everywhere, attention to detail in every nook and corner, an attentive and competent crew, and the company of her two boys and husband for a much-needed get-away, Eliza spent most of the trip horribly seasick with her head hanging over the side of the boat. She was cold, miserable, and very, very nauseous. No amount of motion sickness pills (administered too late in the game) or ginger tablets could quiet her stomach. When the waters and her tummy finally calmed down, Eliza spent quite a bit of time at the hot beverage station set up at all times for the passengers. Tea would be all she could tolerate for a bit. The drink station had a practical, mariner elegance she really admired—lots of polished brass appropriate to a sea faring setting, and a wide assortment of teas, hot chocolate, coffee blends, and even broths for the guests. No paper cups or plastic utensils to be found. The beverage station was as well appointed, stocked, and elevated as any found at the best hotels. Even with a weak and traumatized stomach, Eliza appreciated the beautiful, classy presentation of it all. She just might take the idea back home with her. So, the trip was not a complete disaster after all.

Serve Yourself

WHY NOT TRY making a hot beverage station during winter, à la bed and breakfast, high-end accommodation, or ski resort?

The Mouse, the Praying Mantis, and the Dustbuster

Some mornings are less routine than others. Today started out like most—drink coffee, empty the dishwasher, tidy the kitchen. In the process, Simone grabbed her handy Dustbuster, bending over to vacuum up bits and crumbs of toast on the floor and counter. In straightening, she found herself eye to eye with a **very** large praying mantis examining her from its perch on the windowsill. Startled and unsettled by its gaze, Simone unthinkingly turned the Dustbuster on the unsuspecting guest and promptly sucked it into the canister . . . where, none the worse for wear, it began exploring its confinement. Then, out of the corner of her eye, she saw a tiny baby mouse seemingly napping contentedly in the middle of her kitchen floor. Simone took another sip from her coffee and postulated that both critters had inadvertently been blown into her home by the exceptionally powerful leaf blower being used next door—likely scaring both the baby mouse and the praying mantis out of their natural habitat. The mouse was so still she felt certain it was dead, but on closer inspection, she realized it was not. With Dustbuster still in hand, she instinctively turned it on the tiny mouse out of self-defense. Much to her surprise, she realized that now both the mouse **and** the praying mantis were cavorting in the small vacuum, neither apparently injured or bothered by their situation. What a weird and unexpected way to start the morning, she thought as she hastily headed for the front door to release her unexpected guests. She was already beginning to compose the story she would recount for her young neighbors next door when they got home from school.

Through the Eyes of a Child

WHY NOT TRY crafting a children's story from something that happened to you in the course of a day? Something whimsical, educational, or fantastical.

Save Yourself a World of Hurt

Isabella's sister was justifiably upset. Her wallet had been stolen out of her purse while at a school fundraiser, no less, and while it didn't contain much cash, it **did** contain her driver's license, credit cards, medication list, and health insurance cards. Now, all of which needed to be replaced and reported. She had been meaning to make copies of all of those items to record the important information along with relevant contact numbers should something happen, which it indeed did. "Right now, while it's on your mind," she told Isabella, "go make copies of both sides of all your wallet's contents, and when your husband gets home, do his too."

"I'm your older sister, so I am bullying you into doing this," she said. "Save yourself a world of hurt and a lot of frustration, and do it ASAP. You can thank me later. Learn from your big sister's mistake!"

Just in Case

WHY NOT TRY taking a picture or photocopy of everything in your wallet, front and back, and store the copies in a lock box? Driver's license, credit cards, health insurance . . . even your library card.

The Best Two Out of Three

Tessa loved cleaning out and organizing her kitchen drawers and cupboards at the beginning of the new year and after the mayhem of cooking and baking over the holidays. She started with the biggest mess—her utensil drawer, filled with spatulas, spoons, whisks, and so on. She emptied the drawer, vacuumed up the crumbs, and wiped it clean.

Now, it was decision time. She clearly did not need all the contents of the drawer. How many rubber spatulas and wooden spoons did a cook really need? She came up with a very practical rule for deciding what needed to go. The best two out of three: one for daily use and one for backup (or a different size or shape). The rest had to go; given away either to a friend or a secondhand store. By the time the job was done, she could actually shut the drawer with ease and found a lot more space for other things—one-third more space, to be exact.

You're Out of Here!

WHY NOT TRY practicing the best "two out of three" rule when cleaning or decluttering a drawer or a closet? Keep one of any item, and at the most, one for backup. Then discard or give away the third to save space and simplify your life.

What Happens If?

Erika had a **lot** of people who depended on her. It was her lot in life to be overtly responsible, and her family members, both immediate and extended, knew it. Consequently, she had an oversized portion of worry and concern should something happen to her. She'd lie awake at night with a bad case of the imaginary "horribles." What if something happened to her? Who would take care of everything? *Well, why not ask someone?* she finally thought. Or *some* ***thing***? She grabbed her laptop and, in the search bar, typed, "What if something happens to me," having no idea what would pop up. Quite a bit did, of course, but one of the top entries were some books with variations on the title *It's All Right Here.* Erika looked at the listing for a large notebook with sections and prompts to record every bit of information someone would need to know in her absence, from the location of the safe deposit box and keys, to utility providers, and account numbers, living wills and doctor numbers, car titles and insurance information. Erika ordered it immediately, eliminating some of her stress and anxiety, and coaxing her back to sleep.

Think of Your Loved Ones

WHY NOT TRY creating an "It's all right here!" book containing all the important information your loved ones will need after you're gone?

Get "Techie" with Grandma

Becka thought that gifting a playlist of podcasts, audiobooks, or music to her grandmother (who was challenged by such technology) would be perfect for her. She had just moved to a retirement center, and her surroundings and the people were unfamiliar to her. Music and books she recognized and loved could make her feel more at home. Becka knew this from previous experiences of her own. Her friend Emma had just done the same for her grandmother. Emma gave Becka the scoop on how to do it following these guidelines:

1. Choose preferences for:
   - Podcasts: Consider platforms like Apple Podcasts, Spotify, or Google Podcasts.
   - Audiobooks: Audible is popular, but some libraries may offer borrowing options through apps like Libby or OverDrive.
   - Music: Spotify, Apple Music, or YouTube Music are good choices.

2. Create the playlist:
   - Compile a list of content tailored to their interests. Make sure the playlists are not too lengthy, as this can be overwhelming. You can share them directly via email, message, or a shared link. Again, include easy-to-follow instructions.

3. Write down simple, step-by-step instructions on how to access the content. Use straightforward language. Maybe screenshots would help.

Becka then wrote a note to her grandmother with the instructions and offers of technical help. Oh, and a pot of tea and a nice long visit.

Listening and Remembering

WHY NOT TRY gifting a playlist of your favorite podcasts, audiobooks, and special music to someone who may be technically challenged?

A Hoarder of Sorts

Shannon was old-school. And also a hoarder. But not the kind you'd see in a reality show. No, Shannon was a hoarder of good ideas and images, of decor, travel, recipes, gardens. She dabbled a bit in Pinterest and Instagram, but she found them far less satisfying and accessible than the hundreds of tear sheets she had collected over the years from magazines, brochures, catalogs, and even labels. But she had to admit it had gotten out of hand, and she needed to wrangle them into some kind of order, for she did indeed reference them from time to time, for consulting jobs, entertaining, and inspiration in general.

The best kind of gifts Shannon liked to receive were things that solved some kind of problem she was experiencing, and her daughter-in-law knew this. So, for Shannon's birthday, her daughter-in-law gifted her the perfect solution to her paper hoarding problem: a handsome wicker file basket that fit easily on the top of the table behind the desk in her office. With some fun filing and organizing ahead of her, Shannon was thrilled and could now rein in her hoarding tendencies with style.

Tabletop Organizing

WHY NOT TRY keeping a tear sheet file of your favorite pages in an attractive desktop size file cabinet? Think basket weave or faux leather.

Reuse, Recycle, Repurpose

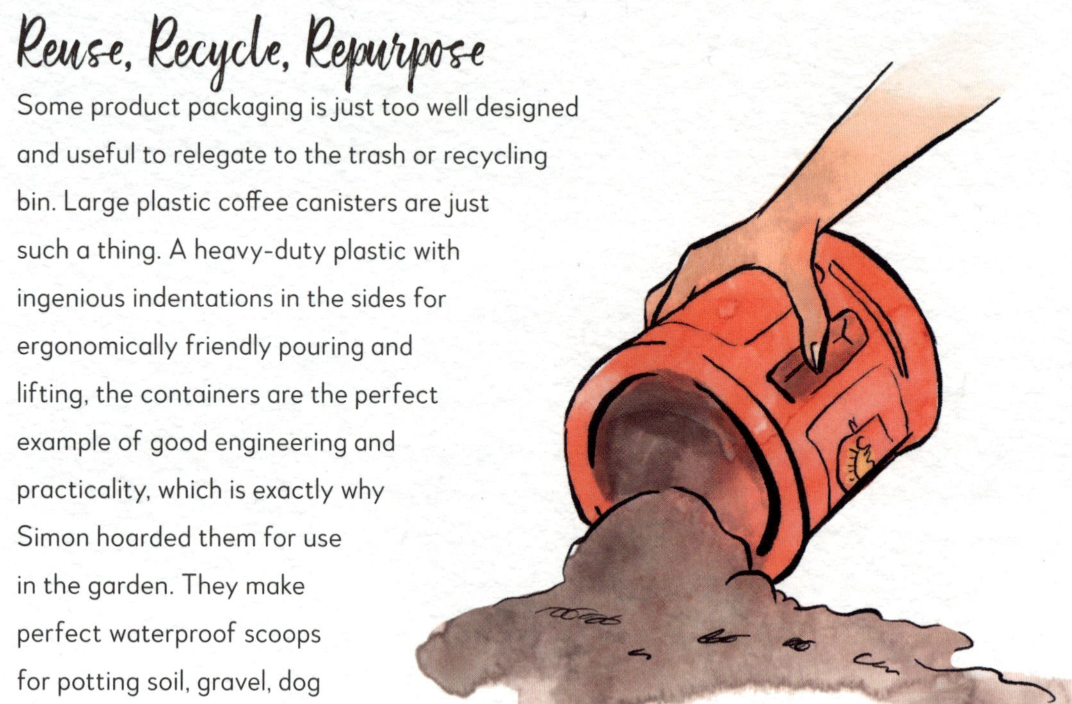

Some product packaging is just too well designed and useful to relegate to the trash or recycling bin. Large plastic coffee canisters are just such a thing. A heavy-duty plastic with ingenious indentations in the sides for ergonomically friendly pouring and lifting, the containers are the perfect example of good engineering and practicality, which is exactly why Simon hoarded them for use in the garden. They make perfect waterproof scoops for potting soil, gravel, dog food, bird seed . . . well, the applications are endless. *Not putting the containers in a landfill was just an added benefit,* he thought to himself, as he scooped another dose of compost for planting his daisies. He could clearly see that this spring he was going to have to up his caffeine intake.

Use What You Have

WHY NOT TRY using empty coffee canisters as soil and gravel scoops in the garden? Don't discard empty containers of anything that might have a special nozzle, unique handhold, or shape that might be just what you need for specific gardening tasks.

And They're Off!

It was so endearing, Wilhelmina thought. Her mother- and father-in-law had been holding an annual holiday competition for years. Right before Thanksgiving, the two of them would plant identical amaryllis bulbs found at their local hardware store and then mark them as to whose was whose. "Let the race begin!" they would declare, and each day, side by side, they would check on the bulbs sunning themselves in the kitchen window. Whichever bulb bloomed first was declared the winner and its human winner had to then take the other to breakfast at the local diner. Fortunately, to her knowledge, it never got nasty, nor were any performance enhancing "drugs" involved. The drama of the large blooms was reward enough for them both, with or without breakfast at their favorite diner.

Blooming Competition

WHY NOT TRY having an amaryllis bulb "race" with someone before the holidays? Pot up the same variety of amaryllis in similar containers and make a friendly wager on whose will bloom first.

Vera Gets a Haircut

Elsa liked to name certain plants in her garden that she deemed deserved the attention. Consequently, her massive Chinese snowball bush now went by the name of Vera, and Vera needed a makeover, starting with a drastic "haircut." Last spring, on a garden tour in Charleston, Elsa saw a magnificent white blooming tree, spreading its umbrella canopy over the brick wall enclosing the garden. She was mesmerized by its beauty, and amazed when she recognized it as the same species she grew in her own garden: a large viburnum. But this one pruned into a stately tree form, rather than being left to grow into an overgrown shrub. She took lots of pictures and studied the architecture of the trunks and branches carefully. She noted that about a third to one-half of the lower branches were removed to expose the trunks of the plant, and then lots of interior branches and crossing branches were also removed. This opened up the shrub, gave it more stature, and allowed the remaining branches to capture more light and bloom more heavily with larger flowerheads. *Well, this was worth the cost of the tour ticket,* she thought, as she made a note in her tour journal to do the very same thing to Vera when she got home.

A New Look

WHY NOT TRY pruning a large shrub into a small tree? Strategically and artistically removing branches to limb-up and open the structure of the plant.

If At First You Don't Succeed, Try Again

You have too much shade. You have too little shade, but sometimes you have too much. You have bad soil. Your soil has too much nitrogen and too many fungal problems.

She had heard it all from turf experts who tried to help her figure out why she just couldn't grow grass year-round in her front yard. Finally, Liz realized that she was asking the wrong question. Not **why** can't I grow grass, but instead, **what** could I grow in its place that might be happier? She started to do her own research, and before she knew it, a whole variety of alternatives presented themselves. *Even good old mulch would be better than dead grass,* she posited. Now, what goes where, for what purpose, and to what design effect—these were questions that were a lot more fun to ponder. Questions that now had answers and hopefully good solutions.

More Than One Right Answer

WHY NOT TRY using something other than grass as a lawn cover wherever regular turf struggles?

Kindergarten Garden

Mona had gardened for years. She had experienced the thrill of victory and the agony of defeat in a way all true gardeners could understand. She had exulted over a fabulous spring show of thousands of tulips and hundreds of violas and pansies. She had been devastated and barely recovered her gardening mojo after an apocalyptic ice storm devastated her pride and joy—a 100-year-old oak tree that was the very reason she bought her first home and started to garden there. In other words, she had been around the garden block a good number of times, and her fixation with various plants and garden design styles had shifted over the years. But one thing **never** grew old, no matter how many times she experienced it—and it never failed to awaken her inner kindergartener over and over again. It was the sheer excitement and anticipation of watching and waiting for a seed to germinate. Annual or perennial, vegetable or flower, even weed seeds held a special fascination for her. Sometimes in the dead of winter, she would plant seeds simply to see them awaken and germinate. It was a thrill to be able to identify a particular plant or variety when it first appeared and declared its presence as friend or foe in the garden. Indeed, she would even say that watching and waiting for the joy of seeing a sprout was a secret of youth. Hopeful, new, fresh. The very essence of being alive.

Mini Miracles

WHY NOT TRY fostering the thrill of seeing a seed germinate? The miracle of it all is as satisfying and miraculous when you are eighty as it was when you were eight.

Bottomless Performances

What a sophisticated garden it was! Filled with interesting and unusual plants and planting combinations. Ida's favorite thing was the rhythm and repetition of the massive planters running up and down the walkway on both sides of the path to the greenhouse—or was it a true conservatory?—in the distance. She couldn't tell if the containers were aged concrete or a very expensive faux look, but the effect they created was truly stunning. They were all filled with a type of dwarf Honeycrisp apple tree with additional measures taken to ensure their survival throughout the winter. The pots were insulated in some way, but more importantly, the gardening staff had removed the bottoms of each of the pots so the plants could deepen their root growth into the actual landscape while still capturing the grandeur of multiple potted specimens and the drama of the look when they all bloomed and grew in unison. They were horticultural performers performing in linear unison; kind of like the Radio City Rockets in New York City over the holidays. The very idea of this, and all of these bottomless planters staged so magnificently, made her happy . . . and **very** impressed.

Go Bottomless

WHY NOT TRY cutting off the bottom of pots that hold small trees and shrubs? With a bit of help, they can overwinter successfully even in cold climates.

A Red Lip

Most everything, Marilyn thought, could be improved with a pop of red. Gardens, outfits, tablescapes . . . and lips, on occasion. Too much red was not her thing, but the carefully choreographed placement of it, whether in the garden, an ensemble, or decor inside the home . . . well, it could make a space or a composition sing, hitting high notes of excellence that couldn't be reached without it, especially when it was used in harmony with other elements such as like-colored blooms or accessories with color echoes of its tone repeated here and there. Scarlet melodies playing just the right notes. She must remember its importance, she decided, and vowed to include more of it in her surroundings and in her days. *A little bit more color never hurt anyone*, she said to herself, as she looked into her tiny mirror to refresh her red lipstick.

Pop That Red

WHY NOT TRY using a pop of red to jazz up your outfit, your living room decor, or your lips? Used strategically and with restraint, it may be just what something needs to bring it to life.

The Appeal and Luxury of Multiples

When she felt unsettled or out of sorts, Naomi liked to visit retailers that displayed orderly, organized stacks of things. Things like pyramids of rectangular glass canisters filled with pantry staples, or identical baskets marching side by side in holding toys in a child's bedroom. What she really liked were soft goods stores with their piles of color coordinated scarves, napkins, or plaid blankets (some with fringe and some without) stacked on a wooden bench or mounded to excess in a large basket. *The essence and allure of simple abundance,* she thought. Her first new home, though small and compact, would definitely be enriched by such easy luxury. So, she grabbed one of the plaid blankets, in her preferred palette of red at the moment, and took it to the checkout counter, intent on bringing it home and copying the warmth and visual delight of a stack of plaid blankets by the little hearth of her new house. Perfect, pretty, and easy season staging.

Large Gatherings

WHY NOT TRY creating stacks of things, piles of things, bowls of things? Make multiple, but not necessarily valuable, collections.

Change It Up

She walked into the classroom with style, confidence, and panache. The way she carried herself, the way she was dressed, and the way she was accessorized spoke volumes about her self-image and stylistic creativity. Her neck scarf was tied simply but classically. No doubt, on another occasion, it would be secured or worn in an entirely different way that would speak to the ensemble of that situation, of that environment. The woman knew her way around chic, the power of changing up a look by reinterpreting how a scarf or a belt was tied—or not tied. It was clear her artistic strong suit was composition, and her scarves were just one of the accessories in her arsenal. One scarf—many looks—great style and sophistication. Another type of lesson learned.

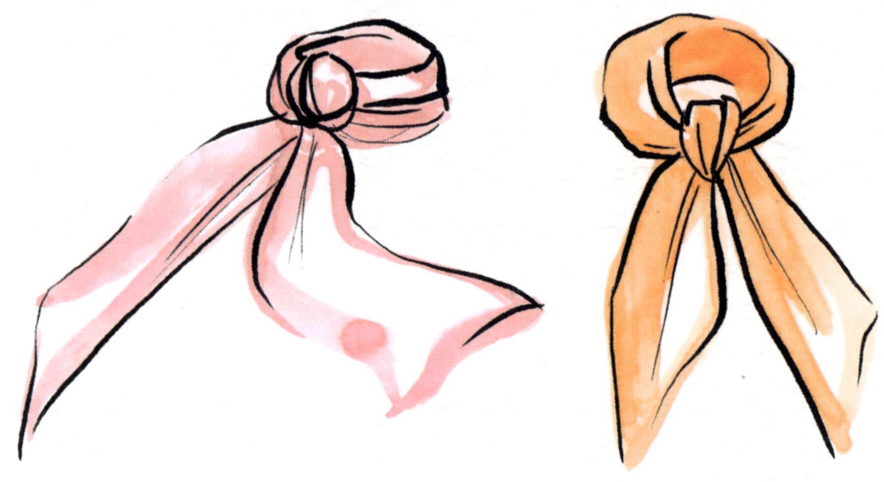

Scarf Smarts

WHY NOT TRY learning how to tie a scarf multiple ways? One accessory can expand your wardrobe in so many ways if you learn some tricks and practice a bit of ingenuity.

Signature Style

Madeleine Albright had her brooches. Jackie Kennedy had her massive black sunglasses. Elle's mother-in-law always wore large statement earrings . . . a personal touch that never failed to delight her young grandchildren. Selecting a signature style element unique to your personality and sense of flair is a wonderful way to be memorable and fashionable. And a great way to have fun and be creative in your personal expression. Consistency and frequency are important when wearing your signature piece, Elle observed, so that others make a strong association between you and your statement piece. No formula, just a fabulous way to stand out from the crowd. Simple, easy, striking. Memorable.

Make It You!

WHY NOT TRY selecting one signature style touch for your personal aesthetic? Do you love gloves, large rings, hairbands, or scarves? What communicates you?

Speak Your Mind with Your Signature Piece

She first noticed it on her grandmother, a stylish woman renowned for her signature hats in the fall and winter. One hat in particular—a stunning fuchsia pillbox—captured her attention. At the center of the front panel, her grandmother had pinned an exquisite brooch of the same hue. It caught the light beautifully, adding an elegant touch, despite being just a costume piece. Even at eight years old, she considered it one of the chicest things she had ever seen. In the summer, her grandmother's winter chapeau would be traded in for a straw fedora. She always looked cool, calm, and collected in any season. While hats may not be as trendy today, another accessory could serve the same purpose and be just as distinctive—perhaps a lovely assortment of colorful leather gloves or a stylish scarf? A chic seasonal wardrobe accessory to synergize your wardrobe. Memorable and **seasonal** and fun—flattering fun, at that.

Say It with Style

WHY NOT TRY picking one statement piece for the season? Try a hat, a coat, a scarf, or a purse. These selections denote seasonal rhythms just like nature and help you appreciate the seasonal changes that other geographies might not enjoy.

A Wardrobe Word Lens

It was a wonderfully simple idea and a fun challenge for them as well. The celebrity stylist was instructing her audience to select three words to describe how they wanted to present themselves to the world: one practical, one emotional, and one aesthetic. "These words," she said, "should be unique to you, your lifestyle, and your attitude towards personal style. Think of it as a lens through which you look at your wardrobe and any accessories . . . and then, make changes to your closet accordingly." Selective, curated, and highly personal was Liza's takeaway. Not one mention of trends or rules or even age-appropriateness. Conscious, intentional creativity was the philosophy behind the practice. How did she want to present and communicate herself and her values to the world? She couldn't wait to come up with her own words, and share the fun and substantive concept with her friends, who would no doubt, have valuable input.

Three-Word Stylists

WHY NOT TRY selecting three words that speak to your personal style? One should be practical, one emotional, and one aesthetic.

Mother Nature Is a Great Gift-Giver

Rocks and fossils shared the same geometry as language, only Johnny and Jamie didn't know it yet. They just knew they were enchanted by the sight of the large quartz crystals bookending the spines of paperbacks in the old lake lodge. The concierge in the lobby, noticing the boys' wonder at them, explained that they came from a mountain peak that once formed a seabed, carved by magma and water and time, and that a small island in the middle of a nearby lake had masses of them. Thus an aha! moment was born in their imaginations and a canoeing expedition to hunt down the treasures was planned. Like magic, their own found crystals were transformed into elegant and impressive bookends as gifts for their grandparents, who would undoubtedly appreciate their creativity, resourcefulness, and sense of keen adventure. A gift from them both with a little help from Mother Nature.

Gifts from Nature

WHY NOT TRY using large stones, hunks of quartz, or large seashells to make paperweights or bookends? Anything inherently beautiful from nature of a certain size and weight makes an excellent candidate. Just add some felt furniture pad protectors on the bottom to prevent scratches.

Batch Hot Cocoa Mix Recipe to Gift at the Holidays

Makes about 12 to 16 servings, 110 to 147 calories/serving

1 cup (86 g) unsweetened cocoa powder
1 cup (200 g) sugar, adjust to taste
2 cups (250 g) powdered milk
¼ teaspoon salt
1 teaspoon vanilla powder, optional
½ teaspoon ground cinnamon, optional

To Make the Mix:

1. In a large bowl, whisk together cocoa powder, sugar, powdered milk, salt, and any optional add-ins until fully blended.
2. Transfer the mix to an airtight container or jar.

To Prepare One Serving:

1. Use 3 tablespoons (6 g) of the mix per 1 cup (235 ml) hot water, or hot milk for extra creaminess.
2. Stir the mix into hot liquid until fully dissolved.
3. Add toppings like whipped cream or marshmallows if desired.

Accompanying mugs or festive napkins are optional.

Cocoa Kit

WHY NOT TRY making your own house cocoa with this recipe? This makes a wonderful gift at the holidays. Use pretty canisters to hold add-ins for a hot chocolate bar with marshmallows, sprinkles, or candy canes.

Peer Pressure

It was ridiculous, she knew. Annabelle was a confident, competent, and successful optometrist. Still, when it came to "room mother" type matters for her second-grade twin boys, she always felt "less than," unable to keep up with the crafty, creative, and time-rich parents of her boys' classmates—until the Valentine castle incident. Quite by accident (meaning she actually had fun helping them) and in a moment of hearts-y inspiration, Annabelle helped the twins create not just the assigned Valentine box for the coming Valentine exchange party, but Valentine **castles**. Castles constructed of varying size boxes, toilet paper rolls (for turrets, of course), and accents using doilies, fast-food meal toys, and leftover Christmas candy. In the eyes of many, the resulting work of art may have seemed gaudy. But in the eyes of her boys and their classmates, even some of the other parents, Annabelle had hit it out of the park, Valentine box-wise. All of the adulation and exclamations about their construction allayed her insecurities and gave her a boost of confidence and parental assuredness . . . in a way no cataract removal surgery ever could.

Valentine Castle

WHY NOT TRY crafting a Valentine castle instead of a Valentine box for your kids' or grandkids' school Valentine parties?

Christmas Wellies

It was such a fun and clever idea, she just couldn't stand it. On the cover of one of her favorite catalogs was a pair of red Hunter wellies with festive Christmas baubles spilling out over the edge. Peeking out were colorful wool socks, a giant candy cane, and a section of fuzzy pom-pom tree garland cascading down over the sides. As a charming final touch, some seasonal greenery was tucked in, making the entire boot ensemble complete. Almost immediately, her imagination went wild with visions of Easter boots, birthday boots, and a baby shower centerpiece of yellow patent leather boots, toddler-sized of course, filled to the brim with daisies. She then ripped off the cover of the catalog and filed it away under "Christmas ideas," with every intention of executing the clever concept in December.

Christmas Boots

WHY NOT TRY a Christmas boot instead of a Christmas stocking? A bright red pair of tall Hunter boots or ankle height boots in a deep green would make a wonderful substitute for a stocking and become part of the gift itself, much desired by gardeners of any age or gender.

Dolly Doesn't Need One More Thing

Dolly and Gregory had just downsized and had put a **lot** of time and effort into getting rid of things they didn't need or want. Their son and his wife had just moved from a large suburban home to an old historic condo downtown and done the same. They told all of their friends and family members with whom they exchanged gifts, that whatever they received, they would prefer that it be consumable, because they didn't want to have to store or find a place for one more thing. Homemade chocolates, spice blends, or even environmentally friendly cleaning products would be welcome. But they didn't really need another figurine or coffee mug, if you caught their drift. Maybe a good bottle of wine, or some of those specialty cheeses they all loved?

Use It Up, Please

WHY NOT TRY buying consumable gifts for "hard to buy for" people or loved ones who have everything? Try gifting anything consumable, homemade or not. Everything from birdseed to bath salts can be gifted and used up happily without being another unwanted tchotchke to have to hide, store, or regift.

The Keepsake Towel

The only thing better than her friend's award-winning chocolate chip cookies was to be given a warm batch of them, fresh out of the oven, and wrapped up in a cotton tea towel. A towel with the recipe itself printed on the fabric, no less. What a brilliant idea. No need to pull out a recipe card; just grab the towel, follow its instructions, and then clean up your baking mess with the towel itself. What could be handier? What made it especially dear to her was that the recipe was a replica of her friends' own handwriting, a regular reminder of the original recipe mastermind. Oh, and on the back of the towel, in a special script? The secret ingredient that put the cookies over the top.

Towel Recipe Card

WHY NOT TRY having tea towels printed with one of your favorite family recipes? Have them made in multiples and give them as gifts to family members, friends, and anyone who has asked for your special recipe over and over. If possible, use the original handwriting of your grandmother, mother, or father as a keepsake your family will cherish for years to come.

Food Brings Us Together

In any book she read as a child, the happiest and most content of scenes was when a family would gather for their traditional Sunday dinner. The preparation for the dinner and the menu where every bit is as important as the actual gathering. Relaxing and cooking throughout the day, together as a unit. One chopping, another sautéing, another baking. Alma had had her share of family Sunday dinners, of course, but nothing quite so intentional and ritualistic. Thinking about Sunday dinners like this made her feel more secure and less alone. Alma had no family close by, but that didn't mean she couldn't replicate the same cozy practice and environment. She had plenty of friends who would love to cook and dine together at least once a month. *Why not,* she thought, *introduce the tradition in her own home monthly?* It would be as much fun to plan and anticipate as to actually gather and eat. Lord knows, comfort food was a priority right now. With that, she picked up her phone and texted all she wanted to include. Getting the first date on the calendar was a good start.

Won't You Join Us

WHY NOT TRY establishing a Sunday dinner ritual with friends or nearby family? It's especially valuable for empty nesters and those living solo.

Charley Steals an Idea

She liked to sit at the bar when treating herself to lunch at a restaurant right near some of her favorite shops. She liked seeing the trays of fresh microgreens sitting there for salad garnishing, and she also liked the restaurant's clever use of different materials for their place settings, like using 5 x ¾ inch (13 x 2 cm) strips of leather as napkin rings. She was sure they used a sharp utility knife to cut the slit for the end of the strip to loop through as it secured the very subtle gray-striped cotton napkins. It was another signature touch of the place she never failed to enjoy on each visit. She liked the ensemble so much, in fact, she had copied the idea for her own dining table, and even gifted a homemade set for gifts on occasion. Handsome and clever with just a touch of a masculine English vibe. Just her kind of style. She was so pleased to steal the inexpensive, good-looking concept for her own use. Why ever not? Ideas were free for the taking. Especially those with rustic elegance like this one.

A Touch of Leather

WHY NOT TRY using leather strips or cording as a ribbon for gift wrapping or a clever and handsome, earthy napkin ring?

Be Crafty

On the corner of the sideboard in her dining room, Yuki had a large blue and white porcelain bowl filled with the most beautiful matchboxes . . . all of them a carefully crafted gift from her friend Michelle. She had selected beautiful color-coordinated papers to decoupage the exterior of each box. The result was so sophisticated and personalized that clearly Michelle had put a lot of thought, artistic sensibility, and effort into each little gem of a box. Though looking so elevated and perfect, Michell had assured Yuki that the process was easy—requiring only the matches, beautiful papers from almost any source, a bone folder, decoupage glue, and cutting implements. "Plus time, patience, and a good eye," Yuki added. Striking a match and lighting a candle was one of life's small pleasures, they both knew. Yuki was so grateful that her friend appreciated this as well, and took the small joyful act one step further with her artistic sensibilities and meticulous craftiness. And a good dose of her characteristic thoughtfulness.

A Striking Gift

WHY NOT TRY decoupaging custom matchboxes for your home and gifts? Large fireplace matches and traditional size boxes both work.

Elizabeth and Her German Garden, an Oldie but Goodie

She noticed it as she was unpacking the many (too many) boxes of books they had brought with them from the old house—how many of the beautiful aged and worn books had handsome covers in shades of dusty blue of varying intensity. They looked lovely gathered together on the console in the parlor. Their blue tones perfectly captured the essence of the personality and palette she wanted the parlor to communicate. She enjoyed displaying them with great care, according to height and blue ombre positioning, and taking the time to actually look at their titles and not just their handsomeness. It had been years since she had read any of them, if she had read them at all. Consequently, she picked up one that caught her eye and started reading from its pages. It was Elizabeth von Arnim's classic novel, *Elizabeth and Her German Garden,* first published on January 1, 1898. Before long, she was captivated by its humor, charm, and idiosyncratic outlook on life. So much so that she put it by her bedside table and read it in its entirety before sleep . . . feeling very Jane Austen-y in the process.

Classic Reads

WHY NOT TRY actually reading, rather than simply admiring, one of those beautiful old books you have on your shelf? If you are a lover of old books (if not high literature); if you find their bindings, colors, and patina inherently beautiful; if you love their scent and perhaps their provenance, from a family member or admired collector; if you feel your home lacks depth and life without them . . . then this gentle suggestion is for you.

All Is Calm, All Is Bright

In Danish and Norwegian, it is *morgenstund*; in Swedish it is *morgonstund*; and in Finland, *aamurauha* captures the essence of the experience. These expressions literally translate to "morning hour" and carry connotations of the peaceful and quiet moments of early morning that are often cherished for their tranquility and beauty. In Nora's life, this translated into meditation in the morning in soft candlelight and peace and quiet, before the chaos and busyness and noise of the day began. After all, why let all of those beautiful candles and candlesticks just sit there gathering dust when they could make such a valuable contribution to the quality of the day ahead? Even the practice of striking a match to light them made her feel tranquil and serene and in control. Those hygge Scandinavians are a wise bunch.

The Quiet of Candlelight

WHY NOT TRY lighting all those candles you never light in the early morning as you meditate and bask in the quiet? Enjoy the gentle lighting before the chaos and the noise of the day begins.

Ol' Blue Eyes

Emily's dad had the most amazing blue eyes. It seemed that toward the end they got bluer and bluer. She and her brother often caught him gazing into the distance, toward the Great Beyond perhaps, steady, forward looking, with that iconic blue gaze. After he was gone, Emily found herself feeling his presence in other ways: garden butterflies, or robins, or the scent of a pipe or cigar on rare occasions. But mostly, she saw him in the deep blue eyes of others. She began looking for people who had especially beautiful blue eyes, and when found, she always made a point to compliment the owner on them. The hunt made her more mindful of others, she discovered. More attentive to their soulfulness, for who can truly and deeply look into someone else's eyes without seeing something there? Joy or struggle, fatigue or momentary passion? Old eyes or young ones. Man or woman, friend or stranger. Without fail, the blue-eyed person would be flattered, a bit taken aback at the specificity of the compliment, but always appreciative that someone seemed to really see them. Isn't that what we all want in the end?

Sincere Flattery

WHY NOT TRY practicing sincere flattery as a form of mindfulness? Spread kindness and living in the moment.

It's All About Reframing

Dave hurt his back, so he couldn't play pickleball. Gwen's home was being renovated and was a dusty, holy mess. No point in decorating for the holidays. Jamie couldn't renew his passport in time, so decided to go fishing in Colorado instead of Ecuador. Elle was writing a book and had a deadline, so missed out on a trip to Japan with her husband and son. Money was tight this year, so Hilda made a huge pot of chili with cornbread and lots of toppings instead of having her office party catered like she normally did.

And each of them handled the disappointment and setbacks just fine. Because each had schooled themselves in the superpower of reframing the bad into something acceptable if not good or better. Can't decorate at the holidays? Then take a much-needed break from all of that work to savor and really appreciate the decorations of others, even at the mall and in restaurants. Can't go to Ecuador? Well, then you've saved a lot of money and airline travel points. Hurt your back? Well, when was the last time you didn't feel guilty about lying in bed all day reading or binging on your favorite Netflix series? Plus, your wife and son hadn't been quite that attentive in a very long time. Of course, sometimes the reframing practice needs rebooting every morning to ensure it is working properly. But that's okay too. You'll have a lot more experience next time this superpower needs to kick in.

Look at It This Way

WHY NOT TRY embracing and reveling in that which cannot be done? Reframe obstacles or setbacks by looking at them differently, sometimes even with positivity.

Valuable Collection Built over Time

Perspicacity. That was her first word. At least, it was the first word she ever decided with conviction was worthy of being collectible. One worth recording, mulling over, using, and appreciating. Plus, she liked the way it rolled off her tongue. She knew of others who collected quotes or metaphors; sometimes, they even matched the quotes and metaphors to sketches or photographs. But Sophie? Sophie just liked certain words. She liked the sound of them; she liked the meaning of them; she liked the way they felt on her tongue. Some words, because she had grapheme-color synesthesia, even had color profiles that appealed to her. She remembered what her grandmother, an English teacher, had once told her: that words, like good china and crystal, should be used frequently—not reserved for special occasions only. Truly, words can be treasured possessions, she had been taught. And she was amassing a valuable collection.

Wordsmith

WHY NOT TRY collecting words, quotes, and metaphors? Record terms and phrases that have special meaning to you.

Dreams and Enduring Relationships

Cora hadn't thought of her old boss in quite some time, though they did stay in touch sporadically to wish each other happy birthday—something novel in and of itself. She was in her early twenties when she went to work for the company, and her boss in her forties. Still, they had respect for one another, shared certain stylistic sensibilities, and bonded on some level. Cora was only at that company a short time, but her relationship with this influential mentor endured well into the future, even after they had **both** moved on to other employment and other geographies, retired and aged. Their relationship had always been a source of comfort and security for her; maybe for them both. She had no idea what triggered the dream, but it made her feel warm and happy when she woke. Consequently, she decided to pick up the phone that morning, and call her mentor to let her know about the dream, and just how much she had influenced Cora's work ethic and attitudes. Needless to say, her former boss, now in her mid-seventies, was thrilled. She was touched. She was surprised. All good things, Cora thought, all stemming from a dream and a simple phone call.

Pleasant Dreams

WHY NOT TRY letting someone know you dreamed about them? It shows that they are in your thoughts, that they played a role in your life somehow, and that they are remembered.

Annual Expression

It had become a ritual for Holly and her friend Deb. They had been doing the practice long before it became popular on podcasts and in self-help books. It was a tradition for the two of them to get together at the end of the year and announce the selection of their word for the coming 365 days. Of course, there was a lot of research and forethought put into the ultimate decision. It was a process that took time, not an epiphany that happened instantaneously. That one word had to preferably have multiple layers of meeting that addressed certain things. Aspiration, motivation, introspection, relevance to stage of life. It was the vocabulary lens through which decisions would be made, and priorities would be established. Sometimes, Holly and Deb even came up with words for each other. Holly loved the substance of the
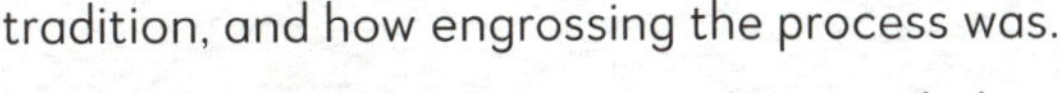
tradition, and how engrossing the process was. Maybe, she thought, this year, they needed to memorialize it in some way. Maybe a bracelet, or maybe a needlepoint ornament

with the word and the year. Its expression could be a creative way to reinforce its message. Just one more fun thing to discuss when they meet to make their big announcements.

Word of the Year

WHY NOT TRY selecting a word of the year? Let it inform the trajectory of your days and months and let it be a lens through which you look at the next 365 days. Your word for the coming year will be . . .

Put Things in Perspective

Jamie was stressed to the max. The project he was working on was over budget, behind schedule, and morale crushing. Before he even had a chance to complain to his wife, she came in the door distraught and in tears. Tay worked in a pediatric oncology unity and over the past week, they had lost two very young patients. Despite all of their life-sustaining efforts, there was nothing more that could be done. Jamie hugged her and drew her a hot bath. Then he headed for his office and a much-needed attitude adjustment. On a sheet of notebook paper, he wrote in large letters, "AIN'T NOBODY DYIN' HERE, MAN! KEEP THINGS IN PERSPECTIVE!"

And so he did. Unlike some things, budgets could be adjusted, people could be patient, and spirits could be lifted. Feeling more in control, with a great deal less self-pity, he started making a list of constructive options for his beleaguered project while making his wife a cup of chamomile tea.

All Shall Be Well

WHY NOT TRY keeping things in perspective when a work project or setback has you stressed or overly anxious? Unless it is indeed the case, hang a sign on the bulletin board above your desk that reads "Ain't nobody dyin' here."

Do Nothing

Do nothing. Really. Nothing. Don't even think if you don't want to. Sit on a swing and daydream. Take a nap. Mindlessly stroll through the bare garden or down the block. Do no laundry, cook no meal, put on no makeup. Let your own creativity define your brand of **doing nothing.**

SPRINGING

blooming,
refreshing,
unfurling,
cleansing,
sprouting,
buzzing

The early weeks of spring are to the totality of spring as a bud is to a fully mature flower at peak bloom. Ah! the buzzing headiness of what is to come. Those first days of the year when we can feel, smell, taste . . . **know** . . . that yes, spring, indeed, finally, is coming. Perhaps already arrived—depending on where we live relative to the spring equilux, that magical, mystical solar symmetry when day equals night, and the sun sits squarely above the equator. We are giddy in anticipation of **all** of it . . . in those most welcome days of the year. Just as that unblemished perfect bud presages color in bloom and gray turning green, so do these early days hint at possibilities—of pleasant hours spent outdoors in play and happy work beneath our perfect skies and equally perfect temperatures. We plan weddings and outdoor dinner parties, conjuring up windless, sunny, warm conditions. The season comes in like a lion, retreats like a lamb, not once, but over and over again, sometimes in the course of a day. Cold and blustery one day, then deliciously warm the following, and sometimes catastrophically and destructively frigid or prematurely scorching the next. Spring, I think, is the ficklest season of all.

I think that is one of the reasons we love it so much. It may snow on the tulips, but there is a high probability of jellybeans and baskets and bonnets come rain or shine. If not on that day, then quite possibly, tomorrow, we hope. If hope were a season, it would be spring. Hopefully, the tulips will bloom large and strong, stand straight and tall, and last long. Hopefully, the last days of school will fly by and summer vacation will come soon. Hopefully, it won't rain on college graduation day, and we can celebrate in the backyard. Hopefully, the peach blossoms won't suffer a late freeze, and it will be a good harvest come summer. Hopefully, the winter blues will recede into the past, and laughter and smiles take their place. Hopefully, we will be energized by renewed exercise, refreshed by spring cleaning rituals, cleansed by long awaited spring rains and mesmerized by germinating seeds and bud break. If day equals night on the vernal equinox, then surely hope equals the possibility of romantic seasonal rhythms. The romance of being able to create lives the way we dream they could be. Spring = hope = possibilities. It's the math of our desire.

Housewarming Gift and Presentation

Donna loved the movie, and she loved its sentiment. She especially loved the *It's a Wonderful Life* housewarming gift that she presented to friends. As far back as her twenties, she had adopted the practice as a traditional housewarming gift, modified slightly with a signature touch of her own. How many times had she gifted a basket filled with salt, bread, wine, and a printed version of that very thing? To personalize it, she would always include a fresh bouquet of flowers so that the recipient's home would always know beauty. She loved the gift but perhaps more than that, she loved its ceremonial presentation. It made her feel warm inside, and hopefully the new homeowners as well. A good omen for new beginnings.

For Your New Home

WHY NOT TRY using the house dedication gift from the iconic movie *It's a Wonderful Life!* as your traditional housewarming gift? Print out a copy and tuck it into a basket filled with bread, salt, wine, and a signature product of your own.

Lighting Those Taper Candles

Most do their spring cleaning in . . . spring, but Elizabeth preferred diving into the scrubbing, decluttering, and organizing at the beginning of the year—as early as January 1. She felt it gave her a good headwind going into the new year. An all-too-jam-packed closet was a good place to start, as she wanted to clear out space and use it for its intended purpose: coats and outerwear. A large square brown box sat on the top shelf; she didn't need a ladder to reach it. She had long ago forgotten its contents and was surprised to find a rather handsome silver-plated candelabra inside, an old wedding gift, no doubt. It tickled her to think of it ablaze, and before she even considered whether or not it was "appropriate," she placed it on her kitchen island and filled it with ivory taper candles. It was cold, gloomy, and dark outside, but when she lit the candles, well, the kitchen, her day, even her mood were illuminated—lighter and brighter. She decided then and there that such beauty was right there for the taking and resolved to light more candles that had just become fixtures on tables and mantles. Anxious that she might inadvertently leave them unattended, she set a timer on her watch to remind herself that they were burning . . . and beautifully so, she thought to herself.

Indulge in Candlelight

WHY NOT TRY embracing candlelight? Luminescent tapers, candelabras, votives in cut glass, pillars, and massive multiwick pillars can keep you company at any time of year.

The Unexpected Guests

Emily really needed to keep a guest book to record all the wonderful people who stopped by the cottage to see her garden. Today, she'd had two unexpected groups of people who followed her on social media—one from Germany, no less, who were in her state to visit relatives, and another couple from New York who were there to see a performer at the downtown civic center. As long as they were "in the neighborhood," they told her, they couldn't miss an opportunity to visit her garden in real life. She was beyond flattered, of course, but even more so, was interested in their stories: How they came to be there, tales of where they came from, and differences and similarities they shared with her on so many fronts. Even though she thought many such visits were unforgettable, she knew that over time the details would fade. She resolved then and there to walk to her local stationer and purchase a guest book to record their visits and the details of their garden call.

For the Record

WHY NOT TRY keeping a guestbook? Record guests who come to your home for a stay, or tour the garden, or special visits from young ones on your street or guests at your first party. Capture the moments by capturing the people.

The D.I.Y. Mom

Ella was never one to make her kids' Halloween costumes, extravagantly decorate cookies for school parties, or help the kids with creative science fair projects. But when it came to making the obligatory wrist corsages for her sons' school dances and prom, she had it covered. She used small rounds of floral foam in a plastic disc, available online, with handy slits on the side to insert ribbon. She crafted beautiful personal versions of the quaint practice out of flowers and cuttings from her own yard. She made sure to inquire as to the girls' dress color so she could coordinate the color of the blooms to the hue of the dress. A bit of greenery with a hint of fragrance added to the charm and allure. Even her teenage sons thought they were special. She hoped their dates were as delighted with the results as she was. So delighted, in fact, she thought to herself that she might have to repeat the practice for her mother-in-law on Mother's Day later in the month.

Homemade Prom

WHY NOT TRY making your own boutonniere or wrist corsage? Use wrist bands that have small discs of floral design foam in them. Prom, anyone?

Wrinkles? No Problem

It was a great example of how she liked things . . . perfectly imperfect. Guests were coming to dinner, an informal gathering, but she always enjoyed setting a nice table with cloth napkins, if not a tablecloth as well. Crisp, starched linens would have been overkill, and too formal at any rate. But the napkins were very wrinkled and needed a bit of smoothing to look nice. She was too lazy to get out the iron, or even her clothes steamer, so she grabbed the glass spray bottle she kept under the sink. She knew that a quick spritz and some hand pressing would suffice to unwrinkle the napkins just so. She proceeded to set the table with a loose garden bouquet as a centerpiece, and her perfectly imperfect cloth napkins as a lovely nod to simple, gracious hospitality. Wrinkles? No problem.

Handy Wrinkle Remover

WHY NOT TRY keeping a spray bottle with water handy for removing wrinkles from your tablecloths, napkins, handkerchiefs, and other flat cloth items?

A Timer Can Be a Great Motivator

Harry's desk was a mess. A full-blown volcanic eruption of papers and pens, receipts, photos, and bank statements. He was dreading sorting through it all, but even more, he was dreading the large project he needed to work on after he achieved a clean, orderly desk. But first things first. He needed to tackle the intimidating stacks of disorder to make way for a clean slate and fresh start mentality. He had been procrastinating and just getting started was the hard part. Then he remembered a tactic his son's kindergarten teacher used to great effect: Set a timer for ten minutes and give yourself permission to stop after time is up. He went to the kitchen, found the egg timer, and did just that. Before he knew it, ten minutes had flown by, he'd made great progress, and was motivated and eager to complete the job at hand. He needed to remember to thank Ms. Kelley for her helpful timer tip. Maybe two apples were in her future rather than just one.

You Have Five Minutes

WHY NOT TRY setting a timer to get motivated? Give yourself a time limit to get something you've been procrastinating about completed. Or at least started. See how much you can accomplish in just the spare minutes of a day.

An Ounce of Prevention Is Worth a Pound of Cure

Anyone who lives in Tornado Alley learns the basics: Go to your basement or to a protected interior space of your home like your bathroom. Stay away from windows and doors. Secure and protect your pets. But Lana knew from sad experience that it was also **well** worth the time to protect your lockbox of important papers and materials from natural disasters as well. Damage to your home, psyche, and garden is enough trauma. Lana well knew that having to recreate, locate, and research important documents added exponentially to the stress and trauma. Lana had indeed learned a very hard lesson. Now these valuables were safely stored in a metal, waterproof box in the basement, well protected from Mother Nature's wrath. Trauma, if not avoidable, can sometimes be managed just a bit.

Be Smart and Secure

WHY NOT TRY safeguarding a lock box of important documents kept at home in a secure area, protected from extreme weather events?

Fil de Fer à Poules

She first saw the idea of using crumpled balls of chicken wire as a large flower frog in a flower arranging book from the 1940s. But the idea was new and fresh to her, and a great idea at that. Chicken wire was cheap and easy to find—she found some at her local craft store—and it worked brilliantly to support strong but heavy stems, especially in the large, statement-making centerpieces she liked to make. The hive-like openings were perfectly sized to accommodate both thick stemmed sunflowers and delicate cosmos, both freshly picked from her garden. And unlike floral foam or oasis, she could use it over and over . . . and over again. Such an elegant use for such a humble material. Who, she wondered, was the first to discover this unlikely application? This kind of simple problem-solving impressed her, almost as much as the exquisite flower arrangements she saw in that old book.

Chicken Wire Flower Frog

WHY NOT TRY using a ball of chicken wire as a large flower frog in floral arrangements? Small amounts can be found at craft or hardware stores and can be reused over and over again.

Colorful Reading

Flipping through a *Veranda* magazine, Miki noted once again a decor trend that had become popular: color blocking one's books. Not the silly, impractical decorator-magazine practice of turning all of the books backward so that only the buff pages and not the titles showed, but rather treating your books like works of art and unique and colorful opportunities for display. This was about creating multiple stacks or shelves of books with great attention paid to cover color and hue, texture and size. Plus, it was so amusing—spending time with each loved volume to position them just so. Pyramids of vibrant orange and sunny gold covers placed symmetrically on a sofa table make great pedestals to display and highlight color coordinated objects. Old, dusty, blue-covered titles arranged lovingly in a unit of color on a shelf or a table communicated an aesthetic all its own. Consequently, Miki put down the magazine and went into her study to do more of the same with her own favorite books.

Color Coding

WHY NOT TRY color blocking your books? Try arranging them in stacks or shelves in all one color, or create an ombre effect with gradients of a hue. It enhances the presence of especially beautiful tomes and can even make them easier to find in a crowded bookcase.

Franny's Dip Was Perfection

"Franny, your dip is perfection!" Gavin exulted. "You simply must tell me your recipe." Franny laughed to herself, knowing no such "recipe" existed—just a concoction she had created out of laziness and the dregs of what she had in her refrigerator. Franny disliked following recipes and was the queen of make-do creativity when it came to whipping up something on short notice. She had forgotten about Gavin's cocktail party invitation, and all guests had been asked to contribute to the appetizer spread. An inventory of what she had on hand: half a block of cream cheese, a bit of shredded Monterey Jack, a couple of roasted hatch chilis left over from the pork chili stew she made last night, some starting-to-wilt cilantro, garlic, and the last little bit of some pepper jelly at the bottom of the jar. Out came her small food processor and in went the ingredients. A sample taste told her that a dash of cumin and onion salt couldn't hurt. Another whir and she had the makings of a dip. Now all she needed was a slice of lime and cilantro sprig as a garnish, some tortilla chips, and a nice bowl for presentation. Not bad for a last-minute dip, Franny decided as she packed it for the drive.

Refrigerator This and Thats

WHY NOT TRY using refrigerator remnants to make a unique and tasty sauce or dip? Think bits of cheese, a clove of garlic, some herbs, and whatever veggie scraps you have on hand.

Double the Fun

Tori first started doing it in college when she needed an inexpensive way to decorate her apartment—specifically her bedroom walls. She'd found some wicker furniture, a small chest of drawers, and a couple of side chairs at a yard sale and scooped them up immediately. She loved the look of wicker then and the love affair continued over the years. She thought nostalgically of that first home and the collection of inexpensive straw hats she'd collected to hang on the wall as wall art. It was a way to both enhance her bedroom and her wardrobe at the same time. Important when she was a starving college student, and still important as a way to inject personality and style into her living spaces now. Panama hats hanging in her parlor gave it a grandmother chic vibe, and her leather and felt wide-brimmed hats now used when hiking and gardening gave both a nod to Ralph Lauren chic and a hint as to her and her husband's interests. Easy to grab and go and to encourage an interesting life . . . and good skin protection, she laughed to herself.

Wear, Then Decorate

WHY NOT TRY using hats you actually wear as home decor and to set a tone and style for your inside spaces and interests?

Tackle Future Issues on the Front End

Jenni opened the drawer where she kept her measuring tape, picture hangers, and other such things, and there they were. She felt a bit smug just looking at them. Small, tightly lidded jars stored upright of four different paint colors she used with regularity for scuffed woodwork, chipped painted furniture, and other inevitable damage to painted surfaces. It was the idea of her painter, Bruce, who suggested keeping small amounts on hand for easy touch-ups without having to excavate the original cans from the basement—and without all of the hassle that implied. He told her to cover the surface of the paint with plastic wrap and put it into an airtight jar or squeeze bottle. "It will keep you from wrangling those heavy buckets upstairs from the basement," he told her. *Such a great tip,* Jenni thought. She paid him more, simply for making her life so much easier. And because he was such an overall great guy!

Small Touch-Ups

WHY NOT TRY saving and storing a small amount of paint in small jars to do minor touch-ups on woodwork and painted furniture?

Trash into Treasure

After much internal debate, Flora decided to transform her front closet, now used for coats and miscellaneous life accoutrement, into an entertainment closet. Shelving could hold china, vases, and glassware; a rod would hang tablecloths and other linens. Her mother would've scolded her for not protecting the surface of her wedding china place settings. "You need to put a round of felt in between each plate so as not to scratch the surface," she would have said. With her mother's words in her ears, Flora was now intent on correcting the issue, but had no such rounds in her possession. She did, however, have thin sheets of foam packaging from a fragile online order she just received. *That should work nicely,* she said to herself as she proceeded to cut the nonrecyclable material into plate-size rounds, feeling quite self-satisfied as she placed the spongy circles in between each plate.

Novel Uses

WHY NOT TRY using rounds of felt, repurposed sheet foam, or even coffee filters to protect stacks of china from chipping and damage when in storage?

Hydrangeas Get a Second Chance

Hydrangeas were Olga's favorite flower. She remembered them blooming in front of her Grandma Loretta's front porch and fell in love with their rounded blousiness, color, and old-fashioned loveliness. They had fallen out of floral fashion for a while, but now were in full-blown popularity both in the garden and in the vase. The only downside as a cut flower, Olga discovered, was how quickly and sometimes inexplicably they would begin to wilt. Then Lance taught her this trick: Recut the stem by a couple of inches, remove any leaves, and then submerge the entire flower head and stem into cool water for thirty minutes or more. The flower should begin to revive, he said. Then place it in fresh vase water in a cool location out of direct sun. Obviously, Lance was a hydrangea lover as well, for his technique worked like a charm. It was one she would use over and over again.

Hydrangea Refresh

WHY NOT TRY giving cut hydrangeas from your garden or a florist a second life when they begin to wilt?

May Day Ding Dong Ditch

Sam had lots of older residents on her street. Some widowers, some empty nesters, some infirmed. She did her best to be a good neighbor to them and put smiles on their faces. Spring helped with its beautiful weather and everything in bloom. She especially liked May Day, with its customary small baskets of flowers or treats left secretly at friends' or neighbors' doors. She had been the recipient of several over her lifetime, from small children on the block who had filled tin cans with wildflowers and then left them on her porch table, laughing and playing ding dong ditch in the process. This year she was going to make May Day baskets for the women on her street. She had more than enough blooms from her garden to make several. She found a stash of glass jars in the basement, tied ribbons around their necks to make handles, and then filled each with seasonal blossoms. She put them all in a large basket for delivery. No secretive doorbell ditch though. She knew each neighbor would want to visit with her for a bit when she delivered them.

Doorknob Bouquet

WHY NOT TRY making May Day bouquets to hang anonymously on neighbors' doorknobs? Experience doorbell ditching at its most thoughtful and fragrant.

The Early Bird Catches the Worm

French Blend Rose and Vidal were Amy's favorite blends of tulips from her preferred bulb supplier. The colors, bloom shape, and bloom time were perfect for her garden color scheme, and even though Amy mixed things up each year in her spring bulb plantings, these were staples in her basket for ordering. But Amy had learned the hard way that ordering early—right after she assessed her bulb performance for that year—was crucial to getting her prized selections. These were very popular varieties and sold out quickly. She also knew from experience after growing them for over thirty years that the company she ordered from wouldn't bill her or ship her until fall, just in time for planting. No downside at all to being an early bird with your order. Procrastination will leave a gardener (and a worm!) empty-handed.

Avoid Disappointment

WHY NOT TRY ordering your tulip bulbs right after spring bloom to ensure availability of your favorite varieties?

A Resourceful Gardener

Nick loved puttering in the small garden of his new house. His only complaint was just how tiny the garden was. No room for a proper potting bench, much less a shed. He had a tiny bistro table and chairs in the space but hated having to use them for his messy projects. As he stood there pondering the problem, he looked at his back door with a flash of resourceful insight. If a door on a hinge could hang with stability, why not a shelf on a hinge that could be folded away after use? He could even stain it the same color as the trim on his house for a polished, finished look. The eve of the roof line would protect it from wear and tear when folded flat. Pots, potting, soil, and tools could be stored in a weatherproof box nearby. He immediately grabbed his keys to head for the hardware store, trying to remember where he had packed his drill in the recent move.

Space Saver

WHY NOT TRY hanging a drop-leaf shelf for a foldaway potting surface in gardens with limited space? It can also be useful when entertaining outdoors.

Grow Your Own Boxwood Topiary

Mabel loved her prized collection of boxwood topiaries. Some of them were as much as twenty years old and very dear to her. The smaller tabletop specimens were even more precious to her, primarily because she had raised them from simple stem cuttings taken from her own garden. Now mature, these homegrown beauties were as full and stately as those bought in established topiary form. In fact, maybe she would start some more specimens today. She got out her sharpest hand pruners and snipped off some of the outlying long straight boxwood stems jutting out from the box hedge. Some of the prunings were almost 1 foot (31 cm) long. She stripped off the lower leaves, hunted down her canister of rooting powder, and coated the stems in the white chalky substance. She filled a container with potting medium—a blend of sand, vermiculite, and a bit of potting soil—then carefully inserted each stem cutting into the soil. She gently secured the cuttings into the moist soil, and then put the entire pot into an area where she could keep an eye on it; a place with a small amount of sun and access to water. Given a bit of time and Mother Nature's nurturing, she would soon have rooted topiary starts she could continue to prune and pinch as they grew into the standard lollipop form. She found the entire process eminently satisfying. Perhaps not for the impatient, she thought, but for a true topiary lover it was the best kind of fun.

Make Your Own

WHY NOT TRY starting your own topiary from long boxwood stems pruned off your garden hedge? Take multiple cuttings, as all stems might not take root.

What a Difference a Day and Four Pots Make

Meg couldn't believe the difference it made to the feng shui and comfort of her back deck. She had wanted to make the space more intimate and private, without any major plantings, fences, or other structural elements. Her sister, a garden designer, offered a solution and helped her implement it on her last visit. Using large pots that were sitting unused and unplanted on the side of the house, the two of them created a "surround" around the four corners of the deck using the pots. The space immediately felt like more of a room, with a cozy sense of enclosure and privacy. And that was **before** they planted the pots with tall conical yews underplanted with cascading wave petunias and trailing variegated ivies. *It all just seemed so finished and polished,* she thought, as she sat there drinking her morning coffee. What a difference a day, four pots, and a sister make.

Enclose It

WHY NOT TRY creating a sense of enclosure and intimacy by punctuating the corners of outdoor spaces with large containers?

The Ladybug Fairy

It was dinnertime when the doorbell rang. Rose opened the door and there stood six of her young neighbors, all seven and under, with their parents standing on the sidewalk in front of her home. Laleh, the leader of the happy little group, asked if she and her friends could release several bags of ladybugs, acquired at a local nursery, into Rose's cottage garden beds at peak bloom. Surprised, delighted, and captivated by the children, Rose watched Laleh carefully teach the other children not to be intimidated by her red splotched friends, and each of them helped scatter the round bugs into their new garden home. Rose was absolutely smitten with Laleh's gift, impressed with her thoughtfulness, cleverness, and ability to coordinate the ladybug release party. It was the best of surprises, Rose thought, and she would ever after associate ladybugs with her sweet young neighbor. Laleh, the ladybug fairy of 18th Street.

Fun with Ladybugs

WHY NOT TRY arranging a ladybug release party with the neighborhood children and their playmates? Bags of ladybugs can often be found at local nurseries or even online.

Don't Overlook the Obvious

It was just so obvious. Why hadn't she noticed it, and put it into practice earlier? Now she was aware that it was a crucial element in almost every beautiful garden design she admired, whether in books or even in her own neighborhood. Successful gardens seemed to follow one important practice: Plant more of what works. In Italy, that might mean one thing; in Vermont, well, quite another. It makes so much sense. If something works and is good looking, structurally important to the design, and is easy to grow . . . **plant more of it.** In her own garden, boxwood was the plant of choice. It was low maintenance, adaptable to her soil and climate, and useful as a great backdrop for seasonal color. Another garden she toured recently had an abundance of mugo pines with tall salvias and assorted native grasses. For that home and setting, it was perfect. Repetition hardly made the landscapes boring. On the contrary the garden was harmonious, eye pleasing, and made good visual sense. The lesson: Got a good thing going? Stick with it.

Stick with a Good Thing

WHY NOT TRY planting more of what works well in your landscape? This practice makes a garden more successful, less tedious to maintain, and creates the necessary cohesion and harmony to make it beautiful.

The Real Stuff

She did it every year. It had become a tradition, started when her boys were young and the idea of using nylon synthetic grass in their Easter baskets seemed, well, unnatural. As of course it was. So, each spring she would grow "living" Easter baskets. It was easy enough to do—she just lined their baskets (usually found at a thrift store) with a plastic bag or pot in which she grew a small expanse of grass. She could find the seeds of the perennial ryegrass she preferred in small quantities at a local nursery, or even online. All that was required was a small amount of potting mix, the seed, of course, bright sun, and a bit of regular watering. *A watched pot may never boil, and watched grass seed may never germinate*, she thought, so she would only periodically check on it to look for signs of sprouting and make sure it didn't dry out. Sure enough, in short order, her efforts would be rewarded, and the tell-tale haze of green would appear on the surface. This made her immeasurably happy as did watching the little blades grow. Once growth got underway, the grass grew very fast. She just might have to get out some scissors and mow her little lawn, she thought, before she added the requisite chocolate bunny, eggs, and jellybeans. She was unsure who would be more delighted at the **real** grass nestling the Easter goodies—her or the children?

Garden Thrillers

WHY NOT TRY creating a container lawn in a small tray to sit on a coffee table or as a modern centerpiece. Or surround one of your holiday amaryllis bulbs in a bed of grass as a living mulch. Simply sprinkle grass seed thickly on the surface of soil, covering it lightly. Water it in, then place in a sunny location. Keep it moist until you see signs of germination and then as it continues to grow.

The Scottish Sky

Until she visited Scotland, she never fully realized how much the sky was part of the garden experience. Why she had to go to Scotland to discover this, she didn't know, because she lived in magnificent sky country herself, at home in South Dakota. *I may not have the benevolent gardening conditions that Scotland enjoys, but I definitely have that big dramatic, wonderful sky as a canvas too,* Viola mused to herself. While Scotland's skies gently wept, quietly and with some melancholy, her prairie sky was stingier and louder. Sometimes violent, typically dramatic, and often angry. She loved it, at least when it wasn't being destructive. Ah, the spectacle of her own skies. Beautiful in their own way. Just as Scotland's were in theirs. *So many languages of beauty,* she thought. Isn't it a lovely thing?

Dramatic Backdrop

WHY NOT TRY looking at clouds a different way? Instead of lying on your back watching the clouds pass by and conjuring up cloud imagery, be more literal with those clouds, and examine how they affect the story your gardenscape is telling.

For the Cost of a Pack of Seeds

A package of hollyhock seeds holds such old-fashioned charm and reminded Chloe of her grandpa and grandma. They grew them near the old outhouse on their farm to camouflage it and told her that in the days before indoor plumbing, they would use the expression, "Go visit the hollyhocks" when nature called. They taught her how to make sweet hollyhock dolls out of the flower's buds and a fully opened bloom. She smiled at the memory. The pink hollyhocks always seemed so . . . exotic . . . even when blooming in front of an outdoor latrine. She had always thought them to be magical and hard to grow, given their tall dramatic presence. She picked up the paper packet and began to read the planting instructions, which in reality didn't seem that difficult at all. Maybe she could grow them herself? And when she turned the packet over and saw that they cost only a few dollars, she thought, what the heck?! Even if they didn't germinate, how fun it would be to try. And for a few dollars, it seemed to be a wonderful gardening risk worth taking—into the cart they went.

A Garden Risk Worth Taking

WHY NOT TRY taking a gardening risk just because you can—and because you might learn something new or discover a new favorite variety?

A Garden Accident Becomes an Intention

So many good ideas can be gleaned from simple observation, Jack thought, as he was sprinkling some foxglove seeds into a concrete planter sitting on the brick wall bordering his front garden. Earlier in the season he noted that a foxglove spire with dried seed heads was arching over a large planter holding one of his topiaries. Regular watering and the protection of pot culture proved to be the perfect environment for the tiny *Digitalis* seeds to germinate and grow into good size starts; starts which he then transplanted into his garden to grow on and bloom the following year. Direct-seeding them into the garden bed itself proved too unreliable. Digging squirrels, foot traffic, and varying shade conditions were the cause, he decided. Given the success and vigor of the unexpected topiary darlings, he decided to go one step further and create a dedicated seeding trough specifically designed for such temperamental seedlings. Consequently, he was thrilled with the success of the many foxglove seedlings in the trough. From experience he knew that in another couple of weeks, when the weather cooled, the little darlings would be ready for transplanting to their place in the flower border. Chicken wire cloches placed over them for protection from those pesky squirrels had proven very effective. *So,* he thought, *what shall I try in my trough next?*

Seed Nursery

WHY NOT TRY starting a seeding trough? Almost anything can be tried as an experiment on germinating annuals, perennials, and herbs going to seed in your own garden, or those gifted by others.

Happy Mother's Day

Elle's son was in kindergarten, and it was her happy task to come up with a Mother's Day project and gift idea for the kiddos to take home to their mamas. Her own mother had always been infatuated with Tasha Tudor, writer and gardener extraordinaire, and in a "Tash Tudor" inspired moment, she decided to invite the children to her own garden to make small tussie mussies as gifts and learn a bit about flowers and pollinators at the same time. A wonderful stretch of May weather lay ahead, she didn't live too far from school, and getting them there wouldn't be an issue. She could wrap the gifts with pieces of ribbon she had squirreled away and knew how delighted they would be with the feel of a lamb's ear leaf, the scent of lemon verbena, and the charm of pansies and forget-me-nots. The kids could cut their own stems after some instructions using blunt school scissors, and she would have cups at hand to keep the bouquets in water lest they wilt. To make it special, she might even serve tea and cookies and put out picnic blankets for them. *Memories in the making,* she thought, as she reached for her phone to message the teacher.

Design by Tussie Mussie

WHY NOT TRY designing your garden with tussie mussie bouquets in mind? If it looks good together in your hand, it will look good in the garden.

Finding Comfort in a Fragrance

Jessie remembered fondly a scene from a book she had read in grade school. It was about a lonely orphan girl who was comforted by the scent of a sprig of lavender a kind woman had tucked lovingly under her pillow. Not accustomed to such acts of kindness or affection from anyone, the girl cherished her gray sprig of dried lavender and kept it by her bed (wherever she might lay her head) for years. The tragic sweetness of this gesture greatly touched Jessie, even at such a young age. Consequently, as an adult, when she was in need of comforting herself, or just in need of a little something to make her feel safe and secure, she would treat herself to one special fragrant bloom, placed in a special vase on her bedside table. Should she wake in the night with a case of the imaginary horribles, she knew that the sweet smell of a hyacinth bloom or the delicate perfume of an antique rose would calm her a bit. It would make her feel less lonely and powerless . . . and comfort her just like that sprig of lavender in the book years ago.

Bedside Scent

WHY NOT TRY putting one scented bloom in a vase by your bed to keep you company while reading in the evening, or when you wake in the night?

The Accomplished Gardener's Superpower

It was the nicest compliment she had ever received. As Elle tended to her garden, her neighbor excitedly approached her, announcing that she had witnessed the first sign of spring. Elle asked what that sign was. Was it a robin, perhaps? Or maybe quince or forsythia in bloom? "No," her neighbor exclaimed. "It was something more subtle. It's you," she laughed. Elle was on her hands and knees, inspecting her garden beds for any hints of tulip bulbs breaking through the earth or seedlings that had begun to germinate. A smile crept across her face as she pondered the sentiment. Kneeling in the soil, she searched for the early indicators of golden feverfew, black-seeded Simpson lettuce, and perhaps even some vibrant Swiss chard. Every year, she eagerly anticipated their arrival, having developed quite a knack for recognizing seedlings—a skill she believed every gardener should master over time. *Knowing how to differentiate between a weed seedling and something precious is an accomplished gardener's superpower*, she thought to herself. A skill to nurture for sure.

Gardening Superpower

WHY NOT TRY learning to identify different seedlings in your garden? Determine what is a seed or a weed; a keeper or a loser. The earlier the better.

Squirrels Meet Their Match

Squirrels were the bane of Rita's existence. No sooner had she tended to her prized collection of myrtle topiaries, meticulously primped and pruned to perfection, than a marauding squirrel would arrive, digging furiously in the soil, scattering dirt and debris everywhere . . . her hours of care in vain, as each squirrel assault effectively destroyed the harmony of her orderly tableau. But then, inspiration struck. An idea flickered to life. Why not top-dress each potted topiary with a layer of beautiful pea gravel? She had often seen this technique employed on succulent and cactus plantings, primarily to retain moisture. As she pondered the idea, Rita realized that deterring those pesky squirrels would be an added bonus. She also appreciated the visual appeal of each pot, now tidily mulched in the handsome stones. Before she knew it, she had set to work, applying a thin layer of gravel to almost all of her potted plants. This elegant solution brought her not only a sense of order and control but also left her feeling quite smug as the squirrels moved on to easier digging.

The Brilliance of Gravel

WHY NOT TRY using gravel in all shapes and sizes as great problem solvers in the garden—for mulch, drainage, or as a lawn alternative?

Coffee-Roasted Compost

Joe loved his local coffee shop. He routinely stopped for a double shot of espresso and the amiable company of the barista there who always remembered his order: the espresso with a side order of a freshly baked blueberry scone. But his morning fix of caffeine wasn't the only reason Joe frequented the coffee shop. As a community service, the coffee shop also saved their spent roasted coffee grounds for customers who liked to add them to their compost piles or bins. Joe, being an avid gardener, was one such customer. It made the entire experience of walking to the coffee shop that much richer. *A delicious caffeine buzz and a no-cost composting essential,* he thought to himself as he dumped the black goodness into his composting bin. All in all, a good and very pleasant morning's work indeed.

Free Stuff

WHY NOT TRY asking your local coffee shops for spent coffee grounds to use in your compost pile?

Avian-Inspired Planters

Victoria had so many outdoor container plantings. During a charity garden tour she once held a raffle and had garden visitors guess just how many she had—the winner getting what? A container garden, of course! Most of her pots were concrete and terracotta; she tended to shun plastic and glazed unless they mimicked the look of the aforementioned materials. But truth be told, she would use almost any container large enough to provide room for her plants. Her favorite shape and planter hack, however, was one she had discovered quite by accident. The concrete saucer of a bird bath with a shattered concrete pedestal had crashed underneath an old redbud tree just off of her patio. Undiscovered for a while in the midst of all of the other garden greenery, it had filled over time with enough rotting leaves and dirt and garden muck that it proved to be the perfect medium for small seeds of forget-me-nots and violets to germinate and thrive. Upon unearthing the accidental and very charming birdbath saucer, she realized it made a perfect doppelganger for far more expensive concrete and stone saucer planters. Already equipped with a large hole (the opening on which it rested on the pedestal) it did indeed look and act the part. *What a wonderful and budget-friendly idea*, observed Victoria. What had happened quite unintentionally could be replicated on purpose. *For what gardener **ever** had enough container gardens?* she thought, smiling to herself.

Birdbath Brilliance

WHY NOT TRY using a concrete birdbath saucer for a unique bowl-shaped planter that looks handsome and expensive?

Tiny Spheres of Herbal Goodness

The catalog had her at the word "boxwood." She was going through her most recent seed catalog planning for spring and selecting new easy-to-grow herbs and vegetables. When she read the description of Spicy Bush basil, also called Boxwood Basil, she knew she had to have it. "Small, tidy dome-shaped mounds with small leaves. Perfect for growing in small spaces and containers. It resembles boxwood plants." On the same page she also found Purple Ball basil with a similar description but in a deep purple color. Both seed packets immediately went into her catalog basket. The basil thrived in her growing zone, easily germinated, looked wonderful in beds and in tiny clay pots . . . and appeared as miniature versions of the clipped boxwood topiary balls she had throughout her garden. *Hmm*, she thought to herself. *Maybe two or three packages would be in order for next year?*

Herbal Boxwood

WHY NOT TRY planting Spicy Bush and Purple Ball basil? The fragrant tidy herbs are beautiful in the garden and equally as wonderful when used as a garnish or ingredient in a summer recipe.

What Broccoli and Dahlias Have in Common

Broccoli in a hollandaise sauce was on the menu for dinner tonight. She was already expecting the resistance she would get from her five-year-old son when the veggie was placed in front of him. She also knew that an ensuing lecture on the importance of trying new things and expanding one's world would be on the menu as well. The next morning, when placing her spring bulb and tuber order for fall planting, she recalled her lecture on trying new things when she came to the ranunculi section in the catalog. She had heard they were difficult and temperamental to grow, and even though she adored their vibrancy and appearance, she had never planted them herself. Well, she thought, what was true for her son was also true for her as a gardener. Without giving it another thought, she put several varieties in her online cart. It was never too late to try new things and expand her horizons as well, in both big and small ways. She couldn't wait to tell her son what she had done. Even she, she would tell him, takes her own advice. Learn by taking risks on something new.

Try It, You'll Like It

WHY NOT TRY to grow something you've never grown before? Even if it's difficult or outside of your growing zone, learn and take a risk.

Cybill Shepherd Beauty Tip

Back in her early twenties, when she was still young enough to read *Glamour* magazine, she came across an exfoliating tip she continued to practice well into her next decades. It was a beauty hint shared by Cybill Shepherd, an actress and model of the seventies and eighties (and who did indeed have lovely skin). She said that one of the most important secrets to her beautiful complexion was to use a rough washcloth regularly to remove dead surface skin and make her skin glow without damaging it. Slow, gentle, circular motions when drying your skin after cleansing was a great way to smooth and soften your skin. Well, apparently Cybill was smart as well as beautiful and talented, for her advice was spot on, both budget-savvy and efficacious.

Inexpensive Exfoliation

WHY NOT TRY discovering the many merits of rough terry cloth washcloths in your morning and evening toilette ritual? Expensive defoliants, abrasive cleansers, and retinoids are all fine and good, but sometimes a low-tech solution is the most effective. Just make sure to be gentle.

New Man, New Hat, New Day

Jamie loved to fish in tropical places and liked to look the part when doing so. Being a fisherman and an adventurer was an important part of his personal identity, and having lived a somewhat legendary life, he knew that maintaining an identity at seventy was as important, if not more so, than establishing one at twenty. And like Indiana Jones, he knew that a good chapeau was crucial to the storyline. Despite many hat purchases over the years, from baseball caps to wide-brimmed hats with a neck-protecting sun cape, he never found one that he truly loved and that fit his rather massive head comfortably. So when he discovered a handsome handmade toquilla straw hat, with a turned-up wide brim and a weathered black hat band, that fit perfectly—not too tight, but tight enough to stay on in a stiff Key West breeze—he knew he had struck gold. He wore it while outdoors of course, but also when grocery shopping, walking in the neighborhood, and at pool parties. Each time he put it on, he got something of an endorphin rush. He could almost smell the sea, and it simply put him in a better mood. Who knew a new hat could hold such power over a person?

New Chapeau

WHY NOT TRY buying a new hat? All of those old movies that had a central scene around the main female character's buying a new hat are not antiquated after all. Try it and see what a mood shifter it can be.

Foot Form Meets Foot Function

It was an unforeseen consequence of moving to a new urban area. Sidewalks, wonderfully walkable sidewalks, leading to all sorts of the very reasons they moved there to begin with. Good restaurants, museums, shops, and the public library. It soon became apparent that her daily step count would skyrocket. As would her blisters, Nora thought, if she didn't get more comfortable walking shoes. Before long, she had quite the collection of stylish, yet walkable shoes. The collection grew over time to include not only a good number of tennis shoes, but also walkable loafers, walkable ballet flats, walkable boots, walkable sandals, and even walkable ladies-do-lunch footwear. Comfortable walking footwear for any occasion, or outfit. And quite stylish, if she did say so herself. She had great fun in curating this perfect shoe collection of "good foot form meets good foot function," and even more fun in using them to explore.

Made for Walkin'

WHY NOT TRY starting a wardrobe of stylish, walkable shoes? Comfort encourages movement and exploration. Putting one foot in front of the other becomes a joy and an adventure.

Take Note

It was so cute and so dear; she just couldn't stand it. Most drawings by her six-year-old granddaughter, Dani, were, but this particular one stood out. It was not only the naive, whimsical freshness of their house that captivated her, but its depiction of scale, the look of the garden, and the way their family and even dog related to one another in the image. Every time she looked at it, another layer of sweetness and happiness revealed itself. She loved its colors, the simple lines, its implied messages. Well, she loved everything about it and decided to capture its charm for posterity. She uploaded the drawing to her favorite online printing source and had it used on paper napkins, stationery with their address, and even sticky notes. When the company suggested using it on a mousepad as well, she ordered one for herself and one for her husband. Quite obviously, she was obsessed with her budding artist.

Personalized Stationery

WHY NOT TRY using a drawing your child made of your home as an image on stationery, napkins, and notepads? Create something truly personalized in a very special and memorable way.

Saundra, Her Displays, and Napkinfolds

Saundra loved working at a high-end gift shop in high school, and later for a time in college. She learned a lot about decorating, composition, and working with different styles and background settings. Over time, she became the go-to employee for designing and setting up displays and creating different looks using the products for sale to create miniscapes for different seasons, holidays, and occasions. The shop sold an extensive variety of different china patterns and crystal; Saundra delighted in setting elaborate thematic tablescapes, and in the process, taught herself different napkin fold techniques and how to use them in various ways. She learned to create the swirling spiral fold, the classic bishop's hat, the lotus fold, the fan fold, and her favorite, the tubular napkin roll for picnics and to go dining—any and all she could learn from online videos or books with illustrations. It was fun, creative, and elevated any dining experience. What's not to love?

Fun Folds

WHY NOT TRY learning some new napkin folds to make your tablescape more interesting, fun, and sophisticated?

Housewarming

Tia was so proud of her cousin. He hadn't had it easy. His parents were killed in a car accident when he was very young, and that obviously affected everything. But Hal, an only child, was a special kid. He figured it out. He kept his head on straight. With sizable scholarships, he was able to work his way through college and even save enough to buy a tiny house near campus. Grad school was in his future, and not inexpensive. Tia knew Hal would be really scraping by for a good while, and though he had a new house, he didn't necessarily have the things required to make it a home—like a couch, dishes, and a coffee maker. But he did have lots of friends, and that's what Tia was going to tap into. She invited Hal's good friends, and even some of her own, to a housewarming party to help him get set up. It was a surprise party, and Hal was blown away by their kindness and generosity. New items and hand-me-downs were all welcome. Christmas mugs worked just as well in July as in December, after all. All it took was some beer, pizza, excellent friends . . . and a great and caring cuz like Tia.

Thoughtful Housewarming

WHY NOT TRY throwing a housewarming party for a single friend who is living alone for the first time, either as a first-time homeowner or apartment dweller?

Do What You Love

Florence hated to shop for gifts. She didn't like the mall, supercenters, or even online shopping much. What she **did** like was going to museums. She was a "culture vulture," and prioritized visiting art and historical museums, with or without her grandchildren. They particularly liked the science and space museum and even the nature centers at state parks nearby. The kid-friendly exhibits are adored, of course, but also the museum gift shops with their enticing offerings for kids and adults alike. Florence enjoyed it as well. Then it struck her! She enjoyed shopping at museums and similar spots, so why not do her shopping there? There were ideas enough for everyone, and she could practically complete her list in one or two spots. And within walking distance of her home, no less. *Talk about a win-win*, she thought to herself, and she soon surreptitiously piled up gifts on the checkout counter for the grands.

Visit Your Local Museum

WHY NOT TRY shopping at a local (or not) museum or botanical garden gift shop for birthdays and holidays rather than at the mall or supercenter? Support their cause and get unique gifts for loved ones.

Wedding Gift Giving for Rebels

Barb was a wedding gift rebel. The easy and conventional way to go—selecting a wedding gift off a predetermined registry with the click of a mouse—was not for her. One of Barb's favorite things to thrift and gift were personalized picnic baskets for the recipients. Actually, it was one of her favorite gifts to give and compose, wedding or otherwise. She collected old baskets for just such a purpose, and would then fill a special one with four place settings of thrifted plates, glassware, flatware, and other picnic necessities: cloth napkins, bottle openers, paring knives, and a small cutting board. All were artfully arranged and then topped off with a small bouquet of flowers and a congratulatory, well-wishes note. The originality and charm of the idea never failed to delight the gift recipient. And creating it never failed to delight Barb. Maybe she'd just add a bottle of champagne.

Picnic Basket Wedding Gift

WHY NOT TRY giving a picnic basket as a wedding gift? Fill it with hand selected dishes, linens, and utensils. Coordinate accessories and colors to the season it will most likely be used.

A Hit at Cocktail Parties

Harper was a brilliant conversationalist. Consequently, she was a brilliant guest to invite to any type of gathering: cocktail parties, networking events, holiday fetes, and dinner parties. She was the queen of small talk by not talking small at all. After initial introductions and exchanges of pleasantries, Harper liked to ask questions she found fascinating. Not personal in a way that is offensive, but personal in a way that each conversationalist's response was fascinating to her. And any charismatic person knows that the secret to being interesting is to be interested. And she was **very** interested in some pet questions she liked to ask that were probing and thought provoking. She had two or three of them and kept others in rotation. One of her favorites was "At this age and at this point in your life, **What do you know for sure?"** She knew from experience that asking deep questions like that guaranteed extended, titillating conversation for quite some time. No small talk required. Harper, Queen of Melting the Ice and questioner extraordinaire.

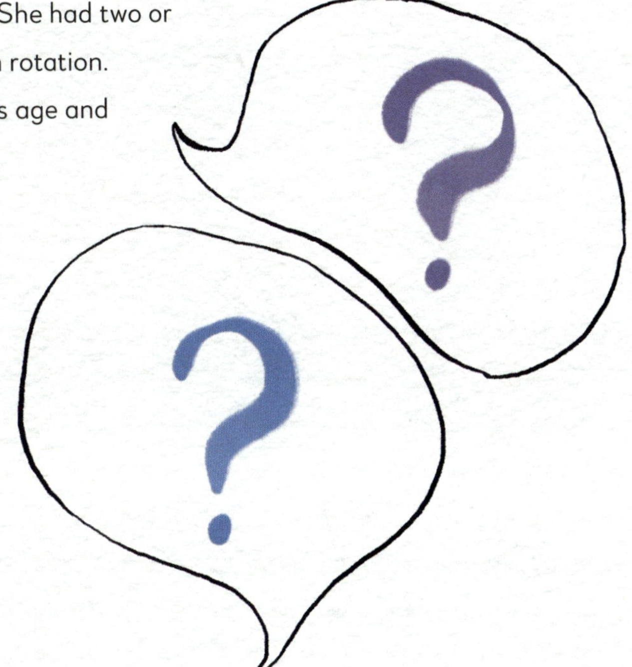

Be Charismatic

WHY NOT TRY upping your small talk game with one or more signature questions you like to ask both friends and strangers? Practice a bit of your own social anthropology.

Wallet, Keys, Phone, and Glasses Keeps the Missus Off Your . . .

Her husband was a good man, and she loved him dearly. But Joe had never been able to leave the house or run errands on the first try. Invariably, he forgot something and had to turn around and come back for whatever was missing. Each time, the wife had to interrupt her activity to unlock the front door (which, without being locked, would always blow open from the wind) and let him in to get the forgotten item. It frustrated both of them to no end, and neither spouse could understand the other's irritation. The problem, however, was somewhat solved when an empathetic friend came up with a helpful little ditty. Wallet, keys, phone, and glasses keeps the Missus off your . . . "Indelicate perhaps," shared the friend, "but it just might save your marriage."

Make It Rhyme

WHY NOT TRY making up a rhyme to remember all the things you need to get out the door? Avoid frustration for yourself and loved ones with this memory hack.

Making the Best of It

Martin wanted a dog in the worst way, but more than that, he wanted a certain kind of lifestyle and a pet simply didn't fit into it. Too much responsibility for a guy with wanderlust who was gone for long stretches of time, and too much to ask of his wife, an obsessed gardener, who loved animals, but between work and home had enough to take care of. Ah . . . but some of the very best things in life, like dogs, could be borrowed or enjoyed vicariously if a guy just put in the effort, he had discovered. He was not above dog-sitting for brief spells, taking neighborhood dogs for walks, and craftily bartering treats for some furry affection and attention. *A good win-win for all,* he thought to himself as he refreshed the doggie water bowl for the day. Having a sidewalk doggie bowl for thirsty pets was a great way to get some affection from a pet, even one not his own.

Think of Our Pets

WHY NOT TRY setting out a water bowl for strolling dogs that walk by your home? It's a wonderful way to meet your neighbors, especially if you are new to the area. It's a thoughtful, inviting, kind gesture that all passers-by will appreciate.

To Heck with Efficiency

There were so many things to move from the garage and out to her potting shed. Stacks of terracotta pots, loads of garden tools, and bag after bag of potting soil, gravel, and fertilizers. It was hot and humid, and she was irritable because she hadn't exercised that morning, so intent was she on crossing this particular activity off her list for the weekend. Out of curiosity, she checked her step counter to see how many steps she had gotten in, despite her lack of power walking that morning. Much to her surprise, all of that back and forth had registered her far more steps than she would have imagined. Well, who knew how productive inefficiency could be. She immediately felt better just by reframing things. She now knew the merits of intentional inefficiency—a very effective, if not efficient, concept.

Intentional Inefficiency

WHY NOT TRY being intentionally inefficient? Trying to do too much at one time, carrying more than you easily can carry, walking faster than is prudent, multitasking—these ostensibly **efficient** practices often set us up for injury, forgetfulness, mistakes, and mindfulness to what we are doing. Consider stopping, slowing down, making multiple trips, and being intentionally inefficient in your daily rounds.

Who Would Have Thought?

Alex tried to garden as organically as possible in both her flower borders and her vegetable beds. Sometimes that meant manually removing unwanted pests like slimy snails and bud-munching worms. Yucky, but at least they stayed put once you found them. Unlike those heinous, rose-destroying Japanese beetles and green-spotted cucumber bugs that flew away just as you had them in your grasp. In a flash of ingenuity, Alex had an idea. She went inside to grab her handy dandy dustbuster, and with a full charge proceeded to vacuum up the vexing critters. She was surprised and delighted with how well it worked and how many she was able to capture in the canister. Just as she was patting herself on the back for her cleverness, she realized she had another problem. Now **how** was she going to dispose of them without them flying away from their containment? Well, she thought, not lacking in confidence, I'll figure that out over a glass of iced tea.

Suck Them Up

WHY NOT TRY using a hand-held vacuum to capture unwanted, flower-munching pests in your garden and on your plants?

Well Done, You!

It was one of the simplest, smartest, most commonsense things her husband had ever done, she mused. Lois asked her husband to have copies made of the key for their new house: one for the kids, one to give to neighbors in case of emergency, and one to have as a hidden backup. When he returned, he proudly show-and-telled the new keys, each one hanging from a different colored spiral wrist bracelet. In and of itself such a small thing, but it proved genius! Just slip one on your wrist when walking around the block or heading to a neighbor's house. Give a bright yellow one to your neighbor where it will stand out easily from all the other keys amassed over time.

No need to carry that heavy car key chain in your belly pack or pocket. Just grab one of the lightweight key bracelets and slip it in your pocket. "Truly, it's the simplest of things—problem solvers—that give us the greatest pleasure," she told her husband. "Well done you!"

Handy Helper

WHY NOT TRY keeping your house key on a stretch bracelet? You can easily slip it on your wrist when taking a quick walk, or supply it to neighbors. Avoid carrying that bulky key ring when it's not necessary.

Save a Special Spot in Your Suitcase

It was the trip of a lifetime, and they knew it. Experiencing Rome as a family, while the boys were still young—well, it doesn't get any better than that. She wanted to savor and remember every minute of it. No doubt there would be hundreds of pictures, but she didn't want to spend all of their time behind the lens. They needed to live in the moment. Inspired by a friend who had done the same, she packed a leather photo album with thick pages of textured paper and cellophane pockets. Plenty of space for the boys to sketch images, record experiences in their sweet handwriting, and tuck in paper treasures like ticket stubs, menus, candy wrappers, and wine bottle labels. She knew in her heart that it would be an heirloom for the ages. It was worth the precious suitcase real estate. And quite a bit of fun, at that.

Family Keepsake

WHY NOT TRY keeping a photo album that has room to write and tuck in mementos on your next trip? Found coins, pressed flowers, and train tickets are just some of the treasures you can keep.

Read Those Labels

What a great and simple nutritional hack, Jake thought, as he wrote down the details his dietician had just shared with him. "Look for two numbers on that nutrition label," she counseled. "The number of protein grams and the total number of calories. This tells you whether or not the protein in its contents was a good tradeoff for the number of calories consumed if you are trying to lose weight." Which he was. But he also knew that protein intake was crucial to maintaining and building muscle mass, and that was a priority for him as well.

So, he had started comparing the two figures. He learned that if you added a zero to the protein grams (for example, 9 grams would convert to the number 90) and if this figure was less than or approximately equal to the calorie count of the food, then it was worth the calories to consume.

Now he had hard evidence that the protein bars that he sometimes ate on busy mornings weren't a poor choice. Their 21 grams of protein when converted to 210 with the addition of a zero was actually only 10 points higher than their calorie count of 200. Almost equal and packed with the protein he was trying to consume. Using this little nutrition hack, Jake just might be able to take off those ten pounds, while not losing muscle mass, after all.

Nutritional Hack

WHY NOT TRY this protein and calorie counting hack when attempting to increase protein while maintaining a calorie deficit for weight loss? It helps preserve muscle mass while still losing weight.

Memorable Decluttering

Finally, Elsie had discovered a way to travel down memory lane while simultaneously being productive and decluttering her digital life. It wasn't enough that her physical surroundings be organized to have outer calm and inner order; now her digital life needed regular tidying and purging as well, she had learned. A photographer friend had shown her this great photo hack. Once a day, a very pleasurable portion of her day, Elsie would spend time going through the album "one year ago" in her cellphone photos app. It was fun to see the photos from exactly one year ago, cleaning out the unnecessary and unpleasing, and savoring (and sometimes editing and using) those that were valuable and useful in the moment. It was tremendously satisfying, and she also knew that she was freeing up precious digital space in the process. *All in all, not a bad way to be staring at your phone as we all tend to do in the course of a day,* Elsie thought to herself, as she continued her scrolling and purging. She truly led a beautiful and rich life, she reminded herself.

A Fun Way to Organize

WHY NOT TRY clearing out your excess digital photos by looking at your "one year ago today" album every morning or afternoon? Or search for a specific date over the years, and savor the highlights, forgotten moments, and treasured images you might want to reuse in some way.

How to Stretch a Dime

Kaye's parents grew up in the Great Depression and found it very difficult to dispose of anything that still had utility or life in it. Socks and mittens, whether brand new or old, that had lost their mate were a perfect example. Kaye's mom used to use mateless socks, especially thick cotton ones, to polish her silver flatware and serving pieces. One for the messy process, and another clean one for the actual polishing. It really worked brilliantly, and Kaye thought it was a stroke of resourceful genius. She was of a new generation that seldom used, or polished good silver, but she did press those single socks and even gloves into service when dusting and even cleaning windows. Not only did it work well, but she, like her mom and dad, discovered the satisfaction of rescuing something from the trash bin, and reinventing it for another purpose. Good and thrifty role modeling to be sure.

Still Has Value

WHY NOT TRY using those "lost your mate" socks to dust, polish silver, remove garden pests, or make hand puppets?

Tori Hearts Trader Joe's

Tori loved Trader Joe's, and it coming to her city had drastically improved her quality of life. The flowers and plants were typically what she was after when shopping there, but there was so much more: great frozen vegetable entrees, great baguettes, great budget-friendly wines, and **great** makings for an easy and impressive appetizer spread. In minutes, she could assemble an impressive hors d'oeuvre tray with TJ's canned dolmas, baba ganoush, and Greek chickpeas with yogurt tzatziki and hummus from the refrigerator aisle, and pita crackers to scoop up all the Mediterranean deliciousness. She added some kalamata olives and fresh cucumber slices (from her own garden), and in minutes she had the makings for a small cocktail party. Vin Santo optional. Next time she's at the store? Coming up with an Italian appetizer combo that's equally as easy, convenient, and impressive. *Yiamas!*

Five-Minute Entertaining

WHY NOT TRY keeping your pantry stocked with items you can quickly assemble for impressive hors d'oeuvres?

SUMMERING

radiating,
basking,
sizzling,
relaxing,
ripening,
browning

Everything in summer is more intense, more potent . . . sun-dried sensations of activity and memories. The smells of summer are strong, powerful, and wistfully nostalgic (not with the delicacy of spring scents). The heavy, humid air of our childhoods was and is filled with the seasonal perfume of chlorine and sunscreen, ice cream sandwiches and barbeque potato chips; the buzzing and itching of mosquitoes and their bites; the feel of a shower or bath, and cool clean sheets to slip into at day's end. Laser sunshine that burns tender feet on hot concrete, but heat that feels delicious as we leave **way** too frigid air conditioning. Contrasts reign supreme in summer. Exhilaration and exhaustion, explosive garden color against a white-hot pale noon sky. Summer—the season that affirms the truth that "the days are long, but the years are short."

As adults, summer seems even more intense, blinding, and powerful. We are not as resilient to the heat and drought as when we were young. Everything is more exaggerated **except** our energy levels in blistering hot dog-day afternoons when the heat zaps daily momentum. We try to live the entirety of our summer in the cool of the morning and the evening.

We harvest pungent basil, crunchy cucumbers, and eggplant, peppers, and tomatoes, cooking them down to their essence and concentrating their flavor. Peach juice drips down chins as we taste for ripeness before baking a cobbler or crisp. The long hours of a summer day can seem luxurious and fruitful, or oppressive and tedious depending on the temperature and the boredom level of school kids on summer break. Summer, with all its bounty and seasonal force, is both yin and yang. Depending on where you live, summer is the best of times or the worst of times. Summer romance runs squarely into a wall of summer realities. Zinnias, meet powdery mildew. Tomatoes, meet spider mites.

Complementary forces and the balance of opposites. That is the pith of summer and we embrace it all.

Hide and Seek

It was her brother's idea. Clara's husband was big on his sound system and it seemed to her as if they had wires, ugly speakers, and woofers, subwoofers and tweeters (whatever that was) everywhere. She hated the utilitarian, messy look of them and the way they stood out like a sore thumb in her traditional home decor. Mart suggested she hide the mess in one or more of the many decorative baskets she had in almost every room. Permeable, large enough, and easy to move, the basket solution was a brilliant one. She couldn't deny it, even though she knew the words "You owe me one" would forever be in her brother's back pocket when he came to visit. She owed him one, for sure.

Hide Your Uglies

WHY NOT TRY hiding speakers and wires in baskets to camouflage their unattractiveness while still allowing sound and air flow?

A Pen Connoisseur

Haley knew her way around the world of writing implements: fountain pens, ball points, felt tips, and even colored pencils. She worked in an office supply store in a small town growing up and had developed some very strong opinions—and preferences—about such things. Let's just say she had a definite POV, one that she shared often in the most novel of ways. She loved to gift "bouquets" of her favorite pens, pencils, and markers to graduating seniors, journal keepers, and aspiring young or old writers. It was a signature touch of hers, these special gifts. And more than one recipient told her they hadn't known what they were missing until they used her favorite gel pen. Who knows? Maybe along the way she had inspired the next James Joyce, Anne Frank, or Charlotte Bronte.

Unique Bouquet

WHY NOT TRY gifting a bouquet of your favorite pencils, pens, highlighters, and other writing utensils to someone beginning to journal, sketch, or take up creative writing?

Garden in Miniature

Her mother had reconciled herself to leaving the family home and moving into an assisted living facility, but still . . . Meg tried to make the space as homey as possible, with lots of family photos, loved objects, and frequent visits bearing her favorite snacks and beverages. Still, her mother desperately missed the beautiful natural setting of her former home and the liveliness of the birds and exploding garden outside her windows. Then an idea struck. On her next visit, rather than edible goodies, she brought her mother a birdhouse and birdseed to hang outside her window, within easy, gazing distance of her chair and bed. But that wasn't enough, Meg knew. So she potted up a rectangular clay container with some of her mother's favorite low-light herbs that would flourish in her window: fragrant parsley, cilantro, rosemary, and thyme. The latter, she knew would be starved for more light, but they could be replaced and replanted as necessary. In the meantime, her mother could enjoy the familiar fragrances and herbal memories she loved so much. On good days, she could even putter and play tending her small garden, Meg speculated. In fact, the joy it brought her mother far exceeded her expectations. Her mother did indeed happily fuss with her small garden, going so far as to instruct the nurses and other residents as to the benefits and culinary applications of her tiny herbal container garden. Quite happily, it proved to be a community garden as well.

Important Indoor Garden

WHY NOT TRY planting a low-light herb garden for someone living in a nursing home or assisted living facility? Provide instructions for maintenance and care.

Pretend You Are Ina Garten

Pretend cooking isn't just for children. Especially if you don't really know how to cook very well, but you love the ceremony, the sensuality, and the ritual of it. Cissy loved watching different cooking shows while puttering around the house, even though she was admittedly lazy when it came to kitchen matters. So, she needed little motivators to entice her. One of her favorite scenes on these cooking videos was when the chef would tear off a large bunch of fresh herbs from a comely pitcher or bowl, then with great knife skills, chop them into submission for the recipe at hand. It always made her kind of sad though; destroying the beautiful bouquet of (no doubt freshly cut) herbs for culinary use. Cissy often composed just such a lovely herb arrangement for her own kitchen, as a motivator to actual meal preparation, or pretending to herself she would do so. In either case, it was a pleasing thing, communicating delicious possibilities and at the very least, a beautiful and fragrant statement on her kitchen island, just like on TV.

Fragrant, Tasty Arrangement

WHY NOT TRY creating fresh cut herbal bouquets for your kitchen counter? Keep fresh-from-the-garden ingredients at the ready for cooking and garnish.

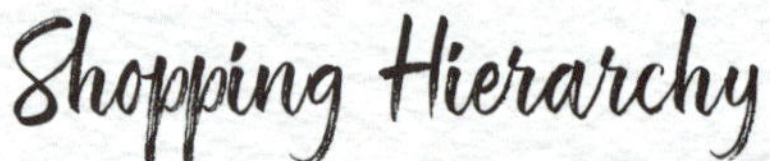

Shopping Hierarchy

It was a shopping practice she had used since in her starving college years. "Style for less" was Paige's mantra, even before the motivation to reuse, repurpose, and recycle was a priority for her when making new purchases. Her hierarchy went like this: before buying new, try to buy or get secondhand. Garage sales were also her friend. Case in point, at an estate sale down the street, Paige had scored the perfect frame for a photo of her niece she wanted to put on display. One far more special than the typical mass merchandiser offerings. It was made of a kind of sculpted wood, handcrafted (at least in appearance), and perfect in style for the image. Plus, she noted to herself, **no packaging,** pennies on the dollar for such an artisanal piece, and she didn't even need to get in the car. *Now, that was a successful buy,* she mused as she walked home with her new treasure.

Thrift First

WHY NOT TRY using a thrifted or secondhand frame instead of buying a new one? There are many advantages: low cost, often unique in style, and vintage materials.

Use What You Have

Noah loved his new house. It was small, but he had big plans. The first time he saw the house with its renovated kitchen/dining room he knew where he wanted to hang a gallery wall. Not a free-form design, but a perfect and uniform grid hanging just behind the banquette. Just like the image of a similar setup he had been carrying around for years torn from the pages of an old magazine. He could just picture it. All but the contents of the frames. His inspiration gallery wall contained black and white images of family members, but he was a single guy still with no family of his own. Unlike many of his peers, he hadn't started a family early. Instead, he had traveled the world, and didn't regret his decision to do so even for a minute, reflecting back on all he had seen and lived and captured on film. Suddenly, he had the answer he was looking for. One of his favorite subjects to record, and experience, were farmers' markets from around the world. Paris to Penang; Aspen to Alberta. He had hundreds of images of these colorful, sensual, diverse places. He started going through his photo folders immediately to select the chosen few that would make the cut for his gallery wall. Perfect subject matter for his new kitchen. They might even motivate him to cook every now and then.

Personal Art

WHY NOT TRY making a gallery wall with a theme that speaks to your interests and conveys your personality? No big budget required.

Summer Fresh

The idea was brilliant, she thought. She saw it on either Instagram or TikTok . . . The chef took a peach out of the freezer, and using a sharp microplane, shaved icy bits of peach in a beautiful golden mound over a bowl of Greek yogurt. Drizzled with honey and topped with toasted walnuts . . . well, it was the thing breakfast dreams are made of. Soon, her brain went wild with knockoffs of this idea: frozen strawberries, fruit that was a little too ripe but still succulent and sweet, papaya, mango. Ah, the possibilities were endless. And how special it would look if served in a champagne coupe. She added it to her list of fun summer things to do.

Freeze in Season

WHY NOT TRY freezing whole seasonal fruits, like peaches and strawberries in the summer and apples and pears in the fall? Use a sharp grater to zest bits of the frozen fruit over yogurt, ice cream, muffins, or your confection of choice.

Baguette Buffet

Going treasure hunting in small-town thrift stores was such a fun thing to do, Gwen thought as she pulled into the parking lot. As soon as she walked in, it called to her—a 3-foot (91 cm) oblong narrow basket lined in burlap—the perfect shape and size to hold an extremely large baguette—(or multiple smaller ones). Immediately it inspired her to throw a baguette party centered around this unique piece. Toppings and summery concoctions were endless. Thoughts of tapenade, hummus, roasted red peppers, soft spreadable cheeses . . . well, ingredients were only limited by a person's imagination. What could be simpler? Jugs of Italian red wine, delectable warm baguettes, and a whole buffet of toppings from which to choose. Before she got to the checkout counter to pay for her thrift store find, a party with great personality was already in the making. Candlelight and a centerpiece of garden-fresh vegetables with string lights and chianti. Clearly, magic lies ahead.

Entertaining with a Theme

WHY NOT TRY hosting a baguette party? You provide the carefully selected baguettes—making sure to include a gluten-free baguette or two—along with a few select toppings and some good red wine. The rest is BYOT—bring your own topping. Extra credit if you serve it outdoors on a red checkered tablecloth with an appropriately Tuscan tablescape.

It's All Up to You

To escape the last of the torrid heat of an Iowa summer, her family liked to head toward Colorado to cooler temps, mountain vistas, and the changing of the Aspen leaves. It was one of her favorite things: the iconic gold of the quaking Aspen foliage against the quintessential blue of a Colorado sky. Oh, how she missed that golden saffron hue when she returned home to her prairie state. She would begin to hunt for expressions of that color everywhere. In the process, she decided to name it her "Color of the Month," and it became a jewel of a tone that she found great joy in seeking out. In fact, she enjoyed it so much she decided to adopt the practice with a new seasonal tone for each month of the year. It was hers to choose, to use, to look forward to each and every month. Plus, there were no wrong answers. Just options.

Make It on Your Own

WHY NOT TRY picking a color of the month each month for one year? Find a hue that speaks to the season, and let it inspire choices you make inside or out.

Late Summer's Bounty

Usually it was far too hot to entertain outdoors in August, but miraculously a cool front had come through, and with family coming into town, eating out in the potager would be ever so pleasant. The fragrance from all the varieties of basils, the color from the peppers and zinnias, and the sweet yellow blooms on the cherry tomatoes climbing the tuteurs would be the perfect late-summer backdrop. *It should even inspire the menu,* Olive thought. Maybe bruschetta, a room temperature pesto pasta dish, and lots of shaved Parmesan, of course. Bottles of chianti for the adults, and gelato for dessert for the kids. Baguettes of bread and a caprese salad—perfect seasonal deliciousness. Checked red-and-white linens and wax-dripped wine bottle candles with an herb and zinnia centerpiece . . . Tuscany on the prairie! Compliments of great weather and the potager's late summer bounty.

Savor the Moment

WHY NOT TRY entertaining around what's in bloom? Are roses at their most fragrant? Are the foxgloves simply splendid? Is the mock orange in full glory?

The Panhandler's Casserole

Tay had lost count as to how many times she had made this casserole, cleverly titled panhandler's casserole, from an Enid, Oklahoma, Junior League cookbook. She usually served it with tortillas, salsa verde, chunk tomatoes, and a hunk of avocado. But she wanted something with a different flavor set, with more texture and creaminess—like a pesto. Then the idea struck her . . . use those mounds of cilantro in her back raised garden to make a cilantro pesto. *The flavor combo would be perfect,* she thought. So, using a basic recipe—nuts, olive oil, garlic, of course, and Parmesan cheese—she whipped it up in her blender. Not too large a quantity, in case it was a failure. But she need not have worried! The outcome was delicious. She might even have to make a second batch. She scooped it into a clay bowl she bought in Santa Fe recently; it was the perfect size and aesthetic. It was also successful. She thought it might need to become a permanent part of her panhandler's casserole repertoire.

Pesto Possibilities

WHY NOT TRY making some kind of unique pesto? Think cilantro, nasturtium, or parsley. Eat fresh and freeze some for later.

A Napkin? A Towel? Or Both?

Lucy liked to window shop in unlikely places. Today, she was exploring a restaurant supply store not too far from her home. It was fun to see all of the commercial-sized appliances, implements, and accessories used in cooking and food service. She especially liked restaurant accessories for table settings: salt and pepper, sugar pack holders, and classic diner coffee cups. But today she had something very specific in mind. On an earlier visit, she had seen stacks of cotton towels, probably to be used for bar service or some such. They had a certain French bistro quality to them, with a red band at the bottom. She thought that with the appropriate stencil and some fabric paint, she could transform these towels into monogrammed, oversized cloth napkins for gifts. She was imagining a large red initial directly positioned above the red line—in multiples, they would look festive tied up with a ribbon and gift tag. Practical, gracious, and distinctive. Just the kind of inexpensive, creative holiday and birthday presents she liked to give. *But why stop there?* Lucy thought. *They're perfect for housewarming, weddings, and hostess gifts too.*

Two-Use Tea Towels

WHY NOT TRY using large cotton tea towels for napkins? Their oversized good looks are practical and often more inexpensive than comparable cloth napkins.

Young One's Library

She just couldn't bear to get rid of so many of them, even the ones that hadn't been read over and over and over at bedtime when her boys were young. Consequently, they consumed multiple bookshelves in her office, and she felt rather guilty at the sight of them. *They really should be in the hands of children,* Dina thought. Then an idea occurred to her. So many children in her young family neighborhood came by for an occasional treat, to visit the butterflies in her garden, or show her their new bike. Why not have her own children's library, right there in her office, all on lower shelves so the little ones could peruse the offerings and then "check them out" with their very own custom-made library card? The idea thrilled her—almost as much, she suspected, as it would thrill the parents and the little book lovers in her neighborhood. A natural attraction if there ever was one.

Home Public Library

WHY NOT TRY Keeping a shelf of children's books for neighborhood kids to borrow? You can make special cards for them to "check out" books from your home library.

Haley's Fridge Saves the Day

Haley hated to go to the grocery store and would do almost anything to avoid it—especially when she felt stressed or tired—but she still needed to come up with their evening meal. She opened her fridge, and it didn't look promising. Almost-empty bottles of salsa, a half block of cream cheese, some wilting cilantro, a wedge of white onion, and some leftover rice. She also had some poblano peppers ready to pick in her raised beds, and a few cherry tomatoes. Suddenly a plan began to take form. She got out her small food processor and dumped most of the contents into the bowl: the salsa remains, the cream cheese, the cilantro, the chopped-up onion, and the last few shakes of the dregs in a hot sauce bottle. After giving it a whir, she tasted, then added some cumin and a squeeze of lime. She gutted the peppers, sliced them in half, then stuffed them with a combo of the sauce, some rice, and a can of black beans. She topped them off with some sliced tomatoes and put them in the oven to roast. Pleased with herself and the now roomy refrigerator, she grabbed a book and a cup of tea, and reveled in avoiding the grocery store once again.

Empty Your Fridge

WHY NOT TRY giving your bottom-of-the-jar condiments a new life in new ways and new recipes? Practice culinary condiment creativity.

Stick It to Them

Caroline loved the opulent floral arrangements depicted in old Dutch Master paintings. Fruits and flowers, vegetables, and often a bee or two coexisted to magnificent effect in these sorts of canvas still-life. The trick to suspending and showcasing the heavier fruit and vegetable elements? Simply puncturing the elements with strong bamboo skewers or sticks of some kind that then serve as "stems" to be placed amongst the other blooms and foliage was the secret. She loved using tiny pumpkins and gourds in the fall, and pears, apples, and citrus around Christmas. Such a simple straightforward technique to achieve such elaborate, complex results. Just her kind of composition; just her kind of ease of execution.

Fresh Fruit Meets Fresh Flowers

WHY NOT TRY incorporating fresh fruit into your flower arrangements using long wooden or bamboo picks?

Gabby's Zucchini

Gabby was simply the best of neighbors. Lucy and her boys, the neighbors across the street, along with some friends, were in their backyard pool, swimming, splashing, and enjoying pool mayhem when Gabby came through the back gate. She was toting a large basket of zucchini, fresh corn, clumps of basil, and some cherry tomatoes. "I'm off to Colorado," she explained, "and I would hate for all of this good-looking produce to go to waste. My eyes were bigger than our stomachs when I went to the farmer's market this weekend. Would you ladies like to take it off my hands before it goes bad in the fridge?" she asked. Of course, Lucy was happy to accommodate and discovered over time that this kind of thoughtfulness was routine for her new neighbor. Lucy had wasted her share of fresh summer produce and refrigerator produce herself and also felt that gnawing guilt at squandering it all. A good neighbor with a good solution. Lucy decided then and there that she would adopt the practice herself. *No more coming home to a stinky fridge and rotting veggies*, she thought.

Nourish Your Neighbors

WHY NOT TRY gifting any fresh produce in your fridge to neighbors before you leave town? Don't let it go to waste and turn into mush you will just have to clean up on your return.

Popsicle Power

It was 110°F (43°C) outside, **more** than hot enough to stock her freezer with every kind of frozen treat imaginable, but Maddie was concentrating on popsicles in the frozen sweets aisle. She knew from years of gardening in sweltering weather that nothing satisfied quite like an orange popsicle, or sometimes a banana one, when taking a stretch-your-back or wipe-your-brow break. Not just for her, but for her yard crew, visiting littles on bikes and scooters, and even the postman occasionally. Popsicles had more than once saved the day when a neighbor child skinned a knee or took a tumble—classic summer meltdowns, for which a cold and delicious popsicle was the antidote. *Summer survival essentials,* she thought as she added another couple of boxes to her cart. Maybe even some ice cream sandwiches for true emergencies.

Popsicle Generosity

WHY NOT TRY keeping popsicles on hand during the summer for your yard helpers and young neighbor friends?

Sometimes It's Not About What You Add, But What You Subtract

Lance was her favorite designer at her favorite florist in town. He just had a way of looking at things. He was also a good businessman and knew that waste in general was not a good practice, even in using flowers that were past their prime to get just the effect he was going for.

He sometimes used dried blossoms because they communicated a floral theme better than fresh ones. And he had taught her that sometimes a sunflower, especially varieties with a bright green or dark black disk at the center, made much more of a statement, an edgy dramatic one, in an arrangement **without** its petals than with them. And he was right. She had seen many examples of this in his work, and she had also adopted the practice with her own wilting sunflowers. Plus, she loved the life lesson in it. There is much beauty to be had from that which is aging and not in the blush of youth.

Floral Editing

WHY NOT TRY using sunflowers in arrangements after the petals have wilted? After removing the wilted petals, you can use the petal-free discs to make a new arrangement.

String Light Traditions

In Ashley's new neighborhood, it was a tradition, an unstated "rule," if you will, that white string lights were strung across the front of the porch or its railing all season long. Not just the holidays or festive occasions, but all year long. The effect was delightful and made the neighborhood seem more friendly and approachable at all times of the year. Ashley wanted to follow suit when she moved into her "new" old home in the historic neighborhood, but outdoor outlets were scarce to nonexistent and getting power to string lights was more difficult than one would think. That is, until her handyman, Ralph, told her about solar-powered string lights that required no electricity and were very reliably powered and lit in their sunny Southern state. Their success introduced her to a world of solar powered products: outdoor candles, tea lights, and lanterns, all powered by the sun, without an ugly extension cord to be seen. Who knew that such things could make her feel more welcome and more settled into her new home? A whole world of sunny solar power opened up to her and her gardens.

Solar-Powered Charm

WHY NOT TRY using solar-powered string lights, pillar candles, and light bulbs for outdoor lighting needs?

What a Guy! What an Idea!

Right by his front door, there it was. A beautiful, mossy, aged concrete pot filled with . . . empty wine bottles. Strategically selected in tones of blues and greens, the empty bottles were placed bottoms up in circular patterns to amazing effect. The hues were perfect color echoes of the seasonal colors Jon used in his garden beds. Their dusty patina in the old pot gave the entire display an old-world Moroccan aura, and their glassy surfaces captured the light magically at certain times of the day. Their display intimated the good times with friends Jon had enjoyed in the content's consumption, and their sheer novelty and creative use made them that much more special. Beautiful "bottle bouquets," a photographer had dubbed them. What a talented eye with a great idea!

Blue Bottle Bouquet

WHY NOT TRY making a bottle bouquet out of interesting and colorful wine bottles to use as a unique garden ornament in a landscape?

Seasoning the Flower Beds

It was genius, really. Well, maybe not genius, but a close second. An imminently practical solution to a common garden problem: sowing very fine seeds like foxglove or poppies without **dumping** said seed all in one place. A place where the seeds then germinated in a crowded mass of overpopulated seedlings, hence causing more work to thin out the little darlings to give them room to thrive and grow. "The trick," a local nursery employee said, "was to mix the fine seed into a base of sand in an empty plastic spice jar, shaking the blend to evenly distribute the seed, and then 'seasoning' the soil with the less concentrated seed mix." *Brilliant, if not genius,* she thought to herself as she left the store, seeds in hand and a new way to plant them in mind. Her weather could be fickle, so she may just have to season her garden multiple times throughout the year to take advantage of rainy conditions and temperatures that made the soil receptive to the seed germination. A fun and pleasant garden chore if there ever was one.

Garden Seasoning

WHY NOT TRY mixing fine seeds like poppies and foxglove into an old spice jar with sand? Shake well and scatter seeds at the appropriate time of year.

From My Garden to Yours

Whether you are six or sixty, she thought, *the urge to pull out a box of crayons to color in a bold black outline of a flower—a sunflower at that—is hard to resist.* She realized this while looking at a coloring book of pop art flowers for sale in the museum gift shop. She immediately thought how fun it would be to translate that idea onto her own custom seed packets, a project she had been thinking about for a while but needed a point of inspiration to motivate her. Well, now she had an image and idea clearly in her head with no further excuse to delay. An online design editor tool to create this kind of thing would bring the seed packets to life in no time. She could already imagine the kids on her block coming by to gather seeds from her garden, and yes, coloring in her signature seed packets in the process, creating wonderful and personal little mementos from her heart and garden.

Personalized Packets

WHY NOT TRY creating your own customized seed packets to save those valuable little treasures from your garden? Add an illustration of some kind on the front—maybe a sketch of your home or a favorite flower in your garden—to make them unique and personal to you. Make sure to include a space to record the name of the seed, when they were harvested, and any other planting particulars you might want to add.

An Herbaceous Love Story

Basil is the scent of summer. If countries had a national scent, Italy could claim basil's intense fragrance. *And my, isn't it also beautiful,* Olivia thought as she overlooked one of the most exquisite plantings she had seen in quite some time. It was a tapestry of basils, each variety in a different rich glossy hue of deep purple or rich green. Each pungent leaf caught the light in its own unique way. This planted marvel was in a garden on the grounds of Villa Le Barone in Panzano, Chianti, Italy, positioned strategically so as not to be too far from the kitchen. Each variety of basil with its distinct flavor, leaf form, and color, would be a key ingredient in some culinary alchemy that would make the guests drool and would scream to the diners, "You are really in Italy now!" She could see the staff setting up the tables—positioned strategically near that amazing mosaic of basils—to set the dining stage. Even if it was just a container version, she knew this was an idea she would have to bring home to her own summer garden.

Living Tapestry

WHY NOT TRY creating a tapestry of basils, if you have the room? Thai, cinnamon, lemon, spicy globe—a world of scent at your feet. Use in cooking and in the vase.

Tragedy and Hope Meet

It was devastating news on the street. One of Sonya's neighbors' sons, who had grown up on her street, was tragically killed in a mountain climbing accident. And at such a young age; only in his early thirties. Before the funeral, other young men who had also grown up in the neighborhood descended on the street before the funeral for collective grieving and remembering. Four of them came to Sonya's door unexpectedly to introduce themselves and visit with her to share memories of playing at her house when they were kids, especially under the canopy of her special 100-year-old oak tree. "It was the largest on the street, if not the neighborhood," they told her. She was captivated by their bittersweet memories of their childhood and their now gone friend's part in those memories. They generously shared them as they looked and wondered at the grand old oak; now more battered and bruised by weather and time, but still grand and majestic in a different way. Then she had a thought. Baby oak tree volunteers sprouted everywhere under its branches from fallen acorns and the magic of germination and procreation. Why not dig up the small tree progeny and share one with each of the young men as a living token of their friendship, their childhoods, and the friend who had played such an important role in it? They all seemed both touched and comforted by doing so, and that in turn made her feel better as well.

Bittersweet

WHY NOT TRY sharing volunteer seedlings from a massive neighborhood tree with those who played under it as children?

Bravo!

Madeline fell in love with a geranium "theater" she had spied in a charming garden in the UK on a recent trip. It was a terraced wrought iron plant stand—three levels—overflowing with beautiful pink and red pelargoniums. As soon as she returned from her travels, she re-created its easy appeal in her own back garden. But now it was the hottest part of summer, and the beautiful blooms were struggling and slowing down. She needed to replace them with something tougher that could handle the brutal summer heat. But what to put in their place? Something colorful. Something tough. Something classic but unique. She looked to her garden library for inspiration and before long, with the turn of a page, she found the solution. *Why not,* she thought, *replace the pots of geraniums with multiple pots of peppers?* She would try jalapeños, banana peppers, poblanos, and fiery red pequin peppers. This checked off all of her requirements and would be perfect for summer cooking and gardening. She loved the idea—she felt quite clever, actually—and it would be perfect in the hot summer months . . . until the geraniums returned for their fall encore.

Great Performances

WHY NOT TRY creating a pepper "theater"? Any kind of multishelf, tiered plant stand makes a wonderful display for any type of outdoor plants. The classic pelargonium or geranium theater can be reinterpreted in the language of peppers or any other vegetable that lends itself to pot culture.

Cut and Come Again

Julia was going to Ireland in two weeks—July 15, to be exact. As much as she was looking forward to it, she hated leaving her garden (which would be in peak bloom by then) behind. The thought of missing out on all those cut flowers pained her. So, when the neighbor girls came by for watering instructions, she told them to cut as many blooms as they liked while she was gone. And their parents too, and also their friends. Then she called her best friend around the corner and told her to do the same before the family reunion she was hostessing. "There will be plenty for lots of centerpieces," Julia told her. "Imagine," she told them all, "that it is your own garden, and you are free to snip whatever you like." They were thrilled. And Julia was thrilled that she wouldn't have as much deadheading to do when she returned. There would be more than enough other chores to catch up on.

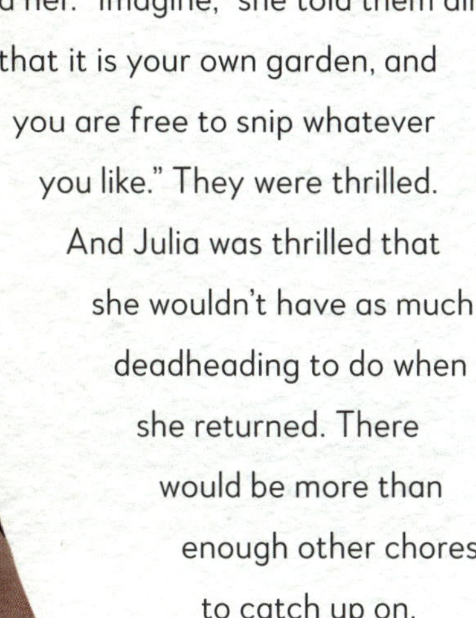

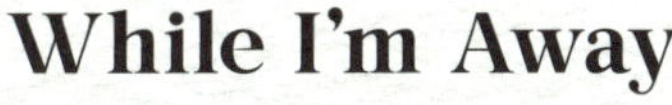

While I'm Away

WHY NOT TRY telling friends, neighbors, and family to cut your garden blooms for their own use while you are on vacation? They can enjoy fresh-cut flowers, and you get free deadheading while you're away.

What Could Be Easier?

It was Ava's first home and her first garden. She wanted to do it justice and make it homey and beautiful. But money was tight (she had just bought a house after all!) and she didn't have a lot of funds left over to create the lush garden she envisioned. Still, friends of hers had shared cuttings and transplants from their own gardens and also shared some easy and inexpensive ways to create more of the perennials and annuals she already had. In some cases, it was as easy as just breaking off a stem and sticking it into the soil to put down its own roots and establish itself as a new player in the garden. But being a new and inexperienced gardener, she was skeptical that it would really be that simple. Still, with a little faith in her friend's advice and the sedum stems she had been gifted, Ava did as instructed and created a border of stems in her new garden bed. Maybe it really **was** just that effortless, she thought optimistically, a sure sign she was becoming a true gardener.

Propagation Is a Cinch

WHY NOT TRY sticking pieces of sedum and other succulents directly into the soil to easily propagate them in place and fill your garden beds?

Spaghetti Garden Gets Its Moment

For over twenty years Amanda had been doing a weekly garden segment on a local TV station. Even after all these years, she still remembered her very first project: planting a large clay strawberry pot with plants, dubbing it a "spaghetti garden." It was the same planting she was doing today and had done many times since. It was a combo of herbs and veggies one would use in making a batch of spaghetti sauce, of course. Heat-loving basils and oregano spilled out the protruding clay pockets on the pot's sides, and cherry tomatoes cascaded out of the top. In very short order, with heat, sun, and attention, it would grow into a full-blown Italian dinner in the making. Beautiful enough to be on TV, and on her own back patio or deck.

Italian Combo

WHY NOT TRY planting a spaghetti garden with oregano, basil, tomatoes, and peppers? Make it a large one with lots of room to grow and mature. This is great for full-sun areas.

Stay in Bed Just a Little Longer

They did it every morning at 6:30. Kara was at a fitness camp for a week, and that's how the day began—stretching in the gym before all the hiking and gym exercise. The daily ritual stressed the importance of stretching to avoid strain and injury. When Kara returned home, she really wanted to maintain her good habits, and discovered something that helped tremendously. Most of the stretches she did at the gym on a mat could be done from the comfort of her bed, **before** she even got up! Not only that; it had become routine for both her and her husband to do them together, stretching in tandem. A few required standing, but that was a no-brainer. Do them as soon as you stand after getting up. It proved to be a wonderful way to establish a good habit for the both of them. Who knew that staying in bed longer in the morning would be such a good thing?

Streeeeeetch

WHY NOT TRY doing those important stretch exercises before you even get out of bed? No leggings or mats required! Get your day off to a good and limber start. You'll be glad you did!

Resourceful Beauty

Tanya looked with dismay at all of the lipsticks she had accumulated over the years. Even after tossing at least half of them, she still had a good number left over, and truth be told, she only used three or four with any regularity. This unnecessary consumption bothered her, especially when she remembered a story her grandmother shared about a prized tube she carried with her everywhere. One tube only, Revlon's Love That Red. She kept it in her purse for touch-ups and a quick dose of glamour when she needed it. She showed her granddaughter how to make a long-lasting lip stain out of the lipstick using a tissue and her pinkie. In a pinch, she would also use it as a blush, using the residue on her finger to give her cheeks a coordinating infusion of rosiness. *That generation was so resourceful,* Tanya thought. Out of necessity perhaps, but a noble practice regardless.

A Dab Here and a Dab There

WHY NOT TRY making a lip stain and blush out of lipstick? Channel your grandmothers and chic women of the past.

Dani Does the High/Low

Dani was something of a nonconformist, but in the best and most stylish of ways. She mixed clashing patterns and textures in her outfits, endearingly named all of her houseplants, and loved to host winter picnics in her local park. And she adored wearing boots, especially her tall Hunter rain boots that she said were as cozy as house slippers. The weather didn't matter; Dani would wear them rain or shine. They were her preferred gardening boots, and even in the dog days of summer, she would wear them to putter in her garden beds. She was also one to garden in flouncy, loose, and light dresses made even **more** charming when wearing that high/low look of the heavy boots and the romantic summer dress. That Dani girl had style, no doubt about it.

Mix It Up

WHY NOT TRY wearing tall garden boots with a flouncy dress? The tension between the rugged and the feminine is surprisingly becoming and comfortable.

Aspen Baubles

It was Tilly's first visit to the Aspen farmer's market. She was overwhelmed and delighted by all of the eye candy before her. Every fruit, vegetable, and flower imaginable, in addition to booths filled with art and exquisite handiwork, was laid out for her enjoyment. As was her way, Tilly headed straight to the jewelry tables laden with hand-worked silver and turquoise. What caught her eye, however, was the bracelet on the arm of the girl behind the table. It had a floral design and sparkle that caught her attention, especially when layered with the artist's other silver pieces on her wrist. When quizzed about the piece, the artist laughed and exposed the underside of her wrist. They were, rather than fine jewelry, she explained, doubled up, hair ties from the store that had an expensive, exotic quality . . . interesting and exquisite despite their provenance. True enough, on her next visit to the superstore for toilet paper and hand lotion, Tilly treated herself to some beautiful wrist baubles . . . which did indeed look especially lovely with the silver bracelet she had purchased from the resourceful artist.

Double the Fun

WHY NOT TRY leveling up your hair tie game so they double as a bracelet or other accessory? Ornamental hair bands are everywhere and can be pressed into service in novel and inexpensive ways.

A Switcheroo

Kat and her sister were going to lunch, and as always, each of them looked the other up and down to approve or disapprove of their chosen outfit of the day. They were sisters after all, and if your sister can't be honest with you, who can? Plus, they both liked fashion and "outfitting," as they called it. It was fun for them and had been since they were little. But today, Kat was more interested in what her sister was carrying than what she was wearing, exclaiming quite dramatically how much she loved her handbag. "I bought it last year," her sister explained, "on sale. And as much as I love it, I'm ready for a change." Kat had an idea. "Why don't we head over to my place for lunch and do a purse exchange? You can pick out any one of mine, and I can borrow yours." And from that day forward, purse exchanges happened regularly, doubling their pocketbook wardrobes and giving them yet another reason to get together—no credit card required, lunch included.

Let's Trade

WHY NOT TRY holding a purse exchange with a close friend or family member? Get the handbag variety you crave without spending any money or buying what you really don't need or have room for.

A Very Merry July

It was sweltering and humid outside. The weather was taking a serious toll on Erin's garden and spirits. The searing heat seemed interminable, with no respite from it for the foreseeable future. To lighten her mood, she grabbed her phone to put on a favorite summer music playlist, but instead, soft Christmas music began to play. Instead of changing it, she let the playlist continue and soon festive, wintery, snowy vibe music began to stream. She let it go on (glancing about to see if anyone was watching and thought her daft) then found herself heading to the basement—a naturally cooler spot in her home—and began to drag out tubs of Christmas ornaments and wintery decor. With the Christmas music setting the mood, she began to organize, edit, and plan for the holiday season still months away. She took note of the wreaths that needed new ribbons and twinkle lights and set them aside to tackle later in the day. She thought that she would head into the ever-chaotic season with these to-dos already crossed off the list. A couple of hours later, she realized how much calmer and cooler she felt with a wonderful sense of accomplishment. All quite by accident! *What happens by accident,* she thought, *can also often happen with intention.* So, she calendared a similar "snow day" for July of the next year.

Take a Snow Day in Summer

WHY NOT TRY taking a "snow day" in the middle of July? Pull up your Christmas and holiday inspiration boards on Pinterest and then head for the basement or wherever you store your holiday decorations. While you are under no holiday pressure whatsoever, go through them methodically, saving and organizing what you treasure and discarding the rest.

Cascading Ingenuity

She needed some topiary for a friend's party . . . a chic woman who recognized the classic form of a simple ball on a stem and who wanted two of them for her outdoor dining table under the canopy of a massive live oak in her backyard. But such specimens were hard to come by, and she didn't want to arrive for the party table preparations empty-handed. Then inspiration struck. One of the many racks of recently unloaded inventory at the garden center held nothing but gallon containers of muscadine grapes. The vines were spilling out, cascading over the shelves of the tightly packed cart. How pretty they would look planted in terracotta and elevated on some old black metal pillar candlesticks she had just picked up at a thrift store down the street. Not the same beautiful form as a topiary, but a different elegant form, nevertheless. As the party had a Tuscan theme, she thought them even more appropriate for the occasion and put two of them in her cart, imagining how lovely the vining branches would look cascading down to the table, illuminated by candlelight, string lights overhead, and a soft evening sky.

Unusual Houseplant

WHY NOT TRY using potted grape vines as a houseplant? The vine may never bear fruit, unless of course you later plant it outside, but no matter. The beauty of its foliage and the gracefulness of its romantic rambling form, twining and reaching, is enough to commend it, inside or out.

Red, White, and Blue

The Fourth of July wasn't one of her favorite holidays. It was simply too hot on a typical July Fourth for her to enjoy the festivities—parades, the picnics with questionable potato salad left too long in the sun, and the fireworks that scared her dog, Goose. Still, she wasn't completely without a country-loving spirit. She had long thought that the dry flower heads of the amazing alliums in her garden—specifically the sparkler-shaped Allium Schubertii—would look spectacular spray-painted in a glossy gold as part of a festive Fourth bouquet. Red zinnias, white pentas, and blue larkspur would set the stage, and the gold allium would be the **Kapow!** ingredient. Secured with a cascading flag-themed ribbon, of course. As she looked out the window at her boys' bikes, she was inspired to hang them from the handlebars, and then went one step further. She hunted down the rolls of crepe paper in red, white, and blue that she had used on a school project for Flag Day earlier that year. She carefully wove them in an appropriate flag-related pattern through the wheel spokes on the bikes. The overall effect was old-fashioned charm, and she knew the boys would be excited to ride them in the parade; hopefully, before the heat set in.

Sheen of Gold

WHY NOT TRY spray-painting dried allium gold and then using them in a patriotic bike bouquet? Flourishes of flag ribbon cascading down with some red zinnias and blue salvias complete the look.

A Pinterest-Inspired Outdoor Entertaining Tip

Daisy wanted to have her friend's wedding shower in Mabel's beautiful backyard garden. Mabel was happy and flattered to be asked, and of course warmly assented, especially when Daisy informed her that other than providing the venue, she need do nothing. **Nothing.** Daisy and her friends would take care of it all: the seating, the tables and linens, the food and flowers. All of it. And all of it fueled and inspired by Pinterest images Daisy had been curating ever since she heard about the engagement. When Mabel expressed concern about the requisite flies and bugs that come with any garden in the summer, especially when food is involved, Daisy said she had that covered too. Another great Pinterest idea: floating a cover of fine netted tulle over the entire table spread to protect it from flies and provide a lovely, dreamy gossamer quality to the event—very much in line with the romantic theme being expressed. Mabel was used to being the older and experienced one doling out entertaining tricks and tips. She was humbled and gladdened to discover how much she had to learn about entertaining in the great outdoors from those younger and more Pinterest-savvy than her.

Stay Away

WHY NOT TRY covering an outdoor table with lightweight tulle to protect food and beverages from flies, falling leaves, and other unwelcome insect intruders?

Zucchini Party

Addy loved her little rural town, and she loved the people in it even more. They bonded over many things: their kids, their local library, their high school cross-country team—and their vegetable gardens. And when it came to their gardens, there was also a bit of friendly competition in the mix: who had the first ripe tomato, who had the first ear of sweet corn, who grew the largest pumpkin. It seemed everyone had a special knack for growing one thing or another in particular. Addy could grow zucchini. She baked with it, and made casseroles and zucchini chips. In fact, her family was getting sick of it, and she still had a lot more coming. Obviously, she needed to give a lot of it away. Just like neighbor Roy had basil coming out of his ears and just brought her several huge bunches of it . . . for which he was compensated in zucchini. They were a thrifty community, and hated anything going to waste. Nella, her next-door neighbor, had an abundance of cherry tomatoes and cucumbers, with the same dilemma. Over a cup of tea, she cleverly suggested that they throw a little summer harvest shindig and exchange and share their excess of green riches with one another. "Great idea," Addy confirmed. "Maybe we could even raise a little money for the cross-country team in the process?"

Embarrassment of Riches

WHY NOT TRY throwing a party for seasonal produce you have in abundance? Too much zucchini, you say? Let's party!

Ballroom Confidence

Truth be told, it was out of her comfort zone, but Joey wanted to dance, and it was obvious she needed to get things rolling. She, along with her husband and other friends, were attending a live performance of a wonderful crooner and jazz band in the ballroom of a grand hotel downtown, and the music was incredibly enticing. Before she could talk herself out of it, Joey beckoned her two girlfriends to get out there with her and sway and dance to the rhythms. As she suspected, soon other couples joined in, including their tentative spouses, now less self-conscious to dance with them in a crowd. Joey even asked others, old men, and young boys and girls to come out on the dance floor with her and share in the fun. No one rejected her overtures, and she could tell they were clearly happy to have been asked to participate in the magical scene, music, and setting. She was also keenly aware of how appreciative the band was that someone had taken the initiative to start things off. Sometimes, Joey decided, acting confidently when you're really not is a good thing; a gift to yourself and others. Being first out on the dance floor was a good metaphor for leadership and an excellent secret of adulthood. Good to know and file away for the future.

You Be the First

WHY NOT TRY being the first person out on the dance floor? It is a gift to yourself and others that communicates confidence, joy, and celebration.

Grief Groceries for Those in Mourning

Matt wasn't much of a cook, but he really wanted to do something for his neighbors who had just lost their beloved Nana. A casserole or cookies were beyond his skill set, but grocery store shopping wasn't. He had spent enough time at their house and with their kids to know what snacks, drinks, and other life staples they were always running out of. He headed to the grocer down the street and piled fruit snacks, cheese sticks, apple juice, and bags of baby carrots with hummus in his cart. He put all of it in reusable grocery bags, wrote a sweet note, and then delivered them across the street. *One does what one can,* he thought. Neighbor looking after neighbor. Even if the caring neighbor doesn't know how to cook.

Thoughtful Market-ing

WHY NOT TRY sending friends and neighbors "grief groceries" when a loved one passes instead of baking a casserole or cookies?

Aromatherapy at Home

The boutique hotel in Napa Valley, California, wine country was just what she and her husband needed after a stressful week of being card-carrying members of the Sandwich Generation. Their kids had been in recent need of much guidance: hands-on demonstrations related to new home ownership challenges. Their aging parents were also due some time and attention, payment to be rendered by tackling intimidating stacks of mail, bills, and delinquent paperwork followed by medication monitoring and custodial life oversight. They happily did both, but a relaxing spa weekend with lots of large and small luxuries were now necessary to recharge their batteries. Little luxuries like a branch of fragrant eucalyptus casually suspended over the shower head made them smile. More importantly, it was an easily replicated indulgence they could copy when they got home, and a nice reminder that caregivers sometimes need time and attention of their own.

Fresh from the Shower

WHY NOT TRY suspending a large branch of fresh eucalyptus over your shower head to enjoy a bit of inexpensive aromatherapy whenever you shower? Eucalyptus branches can be found for sale almost anywhere—grocery stores, florists, maybe even in a bouquet you have been gifted. Alternatively, use a large branch of fragrant rosemary cut from your own garden.

How Do You Do, Tabatha?

The two preteen girls who lived next door were some of her favorite neighbors on the block. She could often hear them with their mother and some of their friends and schoolmates laughing and playing in their pool. On one particularly hot summer day, she went over to say hello and welcome them back from their summer camping trip. She greeted the girls and their mom and noticed a shy, unsmiling girlfriend of theirs standing in the background. What happened next warmed her heart and made her love her neighbor even more . . . the mother quite deliberately beckoned the girl and introduced her with great kindness and formality, explaining her connection to the girls and what a good friend she was. Upon being introduced and momentarily in the spotlight, the unsmiling girl lit up at the kind attention she was receiving. She even seemed to stand up taller at the introduction. *Who knew,* she thought, *that allowing a child to feel seen and important could make such a difference?* After all, we all want to feel special and important—at any age.

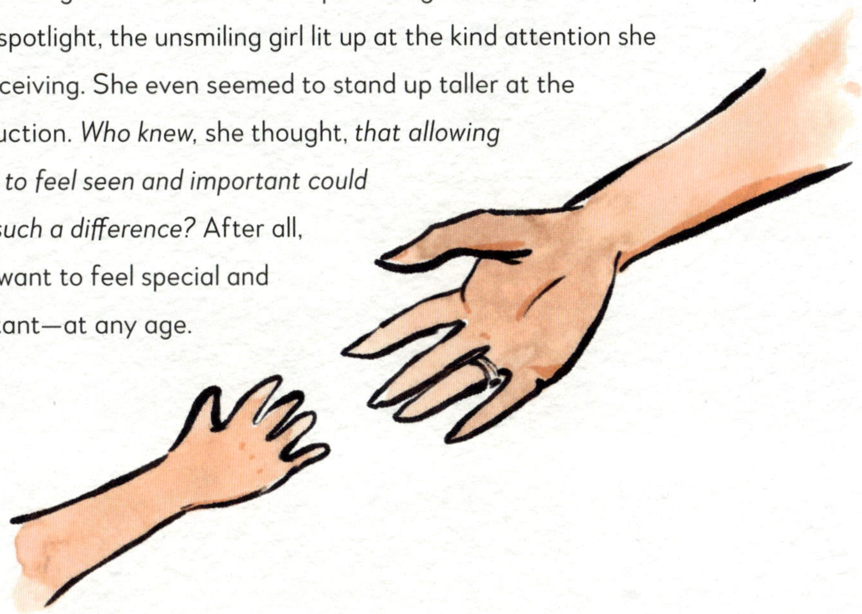

Make Someone Feel Important

WHY NOT TRY introducing a young child with the same intentionality and courtesy that you use when introducing adults to others? This helps elevate a child's self-esteem while teaching them good manners and social skills like looking people in the eye, shaking hands, and ease in conversing with adults.

Look for These Delicacies Wherever You Go

It was an old detective series set in Alaska in the 1990s that gave Constance the idea. *Twin Peaks* had a main character that was always on the hunt for a really good cup of coffee. His own coffee crusade, if you will; he conducted a food pilgrimage of sorts that made his character curious and compelling. She and her husband and sons had taken their own food pilgrimages, researching and documenting their favorite huevos rancheros while in New Mexico, and their preferred peach cobbler in Georgia during the summertime. Diner burgers had their moment on the pilgrimage preferred menu—on a drive through multiple small towns off back roads in southern Wisconsin. Constance never asked for the recipes or hidden ingredients. That was part of the adventure of it all.

Remembering, recording, then hopefully, revisiting important culinary destinations; the thrill of experiencing the dishes again, or the disappointment at restaurant closures or menu changes. In any case, a fun dimension to enhance one's travels, despite sometimes an "enhancement" in one's waistline as well.

Food Pilgrimage

WHY NOT TRY taking a food pilgrimage? Coffee, burgers, bolognese—do some personal research on what your and your family's favorites are and where to find them. Make sure to keep a record of locations.

The Practical Traveler

Blown glass from Prague and Scottish rugs from Edinburgh might be tempting, but not practical as souvenirs of trips abroad. What was practical, meaningful, and would fit effortlessly and chicly into their world back home was a map from each destination they visited. Large or small, old and antique-looking or modern and edgy, all versions would be equally welcome on their gallery wall in the great room back home. And there was always room in their life for more travel . . . and more meaningful souvenirs . . . creating a mosaic map of their life, as well as the geography they had loved and experienced.

Suitcase Souvenirs

WHY NOT TRY collecting maps or stamps as easy-to-pack travel souvenirs? Frame them for display when you return to recall your grand adventures.

AUTUMNING

harvesting,
shedding,
cooling,
breathing,
rustling

What is the sound of fall? In my part of the world, where summers are brutal, hot, and parched, the sound of fall is . . . a long, slow, collective sigh of relief. Everything exhales. All life forms let down their guard against the relentless searing heat of summer, and begin to relax into the lower, gentler angle of the sun—less harsh to all the senses.

Like all seasons, autumn unfolds in subseasons—apple orchards give way to pumpkin fields—Indian summer gives way to first frosts. The softness of light flannel and cotton sweaters succumb to the touch of worn leather jackets and thick socks. We look forward to boot and scarf season and relegate our shorts and sandals to the back of the closet. We are ready, eager for autumn.

As nature's color palette changes, so do our temperaments. External expressions give way to internal ones. The raucous play of pool parties transitions to quieter gatherings around campfires and backyard fire pits. We relax into the cycles of the seasons, embracing the set changes in Mother Nature's script. Nostalgic sounds and scents jettison us back to grade school: the crunch of leaves, honking geese, marching bands, and cheering crowds. We yearn for fresh school supplies and the smell of crayons, no matter our age. We light candles and put on a pot of chili.

Cooler temperatures make us restless. We walk, we nap, we bake, we switch out our wardrobes and bedding and bring out our stack of throws and heating pads. We fully embrace the pumpkin-spiciness of it all. Yet we do not and cannot avoid the seasonal melancholy of shorter days, waning gardens, oppressive schedules, and resumed disciplines of school and work and obligations. What is new and exciting at the dawn of the season becomes tiresome and difficult as the months pass. Consequently, we cheer ourselves with plans and projects for upcoming holidays and the festivities to come—always remembering to savor the scent of smoke, the taste of hot cider, the joy of a team win, and the coziness of it all.

Ah! The individual moments and minutes of autumn. Isolate and relish each sensual one.

Thanksgiving at the Villa

Everything about that Thanksgiving was unexpected. It was unexpected that they were celebrating the very American holiday in a very Italian place—a friend's villa in Chianti. It was unexpected that her friend Patricia had a villa at all. After the death of her husband, Patricia had moved to a Chianti villa permanently—a place her family had rented many times over the years and loved passionately. She now found great comfort, community, and a future in the dreamy place, and had quite unexpectedly invited Kate's entire family to her Italian home for the holiday. Equally unexpected was the way Patricia had crafted her tablescapes. Gone were the rich orange and amber tones always embraced in America. Now her tablescape was luminescent. Bone and ivory colors reigned supreme: white Lumina and Baby Boo pumpkins; pale, colored gourds; delicate, deep green and white kales with their ruffled edges and veined surfaces; ivory candles, illuminating the entire display in candelabras, crystal votive cups, and every height taper in masses of single candlesticks. Not a hint of orange anywhere. Breathtaking, elegant, supremely, seasonal. And yes, very Patricia-esque and very unexpected, in the best of ways. A truly remarkable and unexpected Thanksgiving.

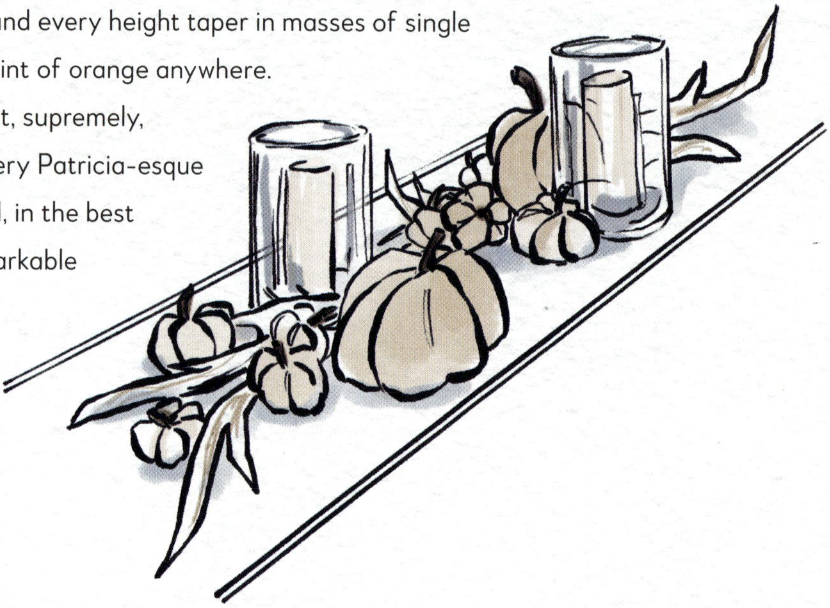

Blanc

WHY NOT TRY creating an all-white fall tablescape with Lumina and Baby Boo pumpkins, antlers, and white candles?

Have a Holly, Jolly, Fundraiser

The tradition for her garden club began when Edith, who hated the mess of candle wax dripping onto her holiday table, crafted small wreaths from evergreen sprigs and holly berries from her garden to catch the wax at the base of her candlesticks. She loved the way the fresh greenery added a festive, garden-y touch while serving a practical purpose.

She demonstrated the charming craft at one of her garden club meetings, where they quickly took to the idea. They loved the dual function of the bobeches: protecting surfaces and showcasing seasonal clippings, all with a nod to the garden and tradition. The use of evergreens and berries not only brought color and fragrance indoors but also provided a fundraising opportunity as well. No bake sale this year. Instead, they would create and sell their handmade candle decor with dripless candles and inexpensive thrifted candlesticks. It proved tremendously successful, and over time, the practice became a simple, practical tradition for holiday decor . . . and garden club fundraising.

Deck the Halls

WHY NOT TRY using stylish glass and natural bobeches made from evergreen material grown right outside your door?

Thomas Jefferson in Santa Fe

They caught her eye even among all the other eye candy at a high-end florist on the west side of Santa Fe. Bone-white okra pods mimicking cast white stone were piled high in an old black clay paellera, both handles of the vessel still intact. Good thing, since it was heavy, hefty, and handsome, the perfect container to hold the magnificent okra Quingombo pods. She recognized the dried hulls immediately, having grown some Cow's Horn okra (*Abelmoschus esculentus*) from seed purchased at the Monticello Gift Shop. Thomas Jefferson was known to be a fan of the vegetable in soups and stews. Whether or not he ever used the dried husks in a decorative way to adorn his table for guests is unknown, though given his cleverness, she didn't doubt it. Inspired by both Jefferson and the Santa Fe florist, she decided to recreate the striking composition in her own home.

Bone-Dry Okra

WHY NOT TRY placing a bowl of dried Cow's Horn or Red Burgundy okra pods into an earthen pot, with or without greenery, to add a seasonal flourish to a coffee table or centerpiece? They are rustically elegant with their bony-white, black-ribbed exteriors, but can take on a sophisticated tone when spray-painted gold, copper, or silver. Extra credit if multiple pods remain hanging like ornaments from a strong dried stem.

Foliar Sculpture

The leaf was simply mammoth. The fabulous sycamores that lined the streets of her new neighborhood were some of the largest in the city, so simply by extrapolation she assumed the leaves they dropped were some of the largest in the city as well. She loved the grandeur of the thought and felt ever so fortunate to be living amongst the magnificent specimens—both the trees and the leaves they shed. This particular leaf was especially splendid. In fact, it seemed perfect, unmarred in any way. The pointed tips were crisp and intact, and it had just a hint of a ripple. Not yet a full fold in its bold form, but a subtle bend in the middle. Just enough to make it seem sensual and interesting, as if it had a story to tell. And oh, the color! A deep, dark coffee and mahogany hue, rich and intense, with graining almost like wood.

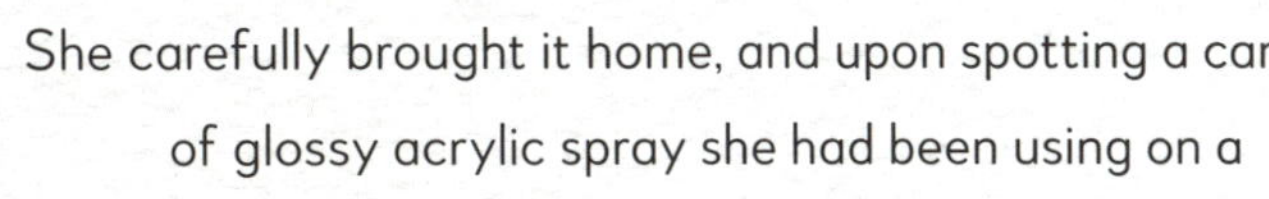

She carefully brought it home, and upon spotting a can of glossy acrylic spray she had been using on a pumpkin project, decided to give the stunning leaf a whisper of a sheen as well. To capture the light . . . maybe even candlelight. It was as spectacular as any sculpture, she thought, and treating it accordingly, she displayed it front and center on her mantle, standing upright in a brass easel for all to admire.

Leafy Sculpture

WHY NOT TRY selecting an exquisitely shaped fall leaf to use as an ode to fall? Find one with personality—maybe with a unique fold or speckled patina; a large unblemished subject, free of holes, tears, or marring. A very large leaf, from a sycamore or a bur oak, for example, makes a wonderful living sculpture, especially when coated with a hint of glossiness from a clear (or even a colored) spray acrylic.

Spooky Is as Spooky Does

She came up with the idea when she saw an expensive branchlike candelabra as part of a store Halloween collection. “How silly,” she thought. She loved the look but knew there was no need to spend good money to get this effect. That day, she started scavenging for interesting, craggy, large and small branches from the massive trees in her neighborhood. Channeling her inner witch, she dragged them back to her home to be spray-painted in dark and spooky tones. She would, she thought, use the largest upright branch to surround and encase the lamppost in her front yard. She could stick it in the ground and adorn it with webbing, furry spiders, and branch-hugging black crows. At the base, she would nestle spooky jack-o-lanterns and ghostly gourds—a display that both Nathaniel Hawthorne and Tim Burton would approve of, all for the cost of a can of spray paint. What a scary good deal.

Get Out the Black Spray Paint

WHY NOT TRY spray-painting a large, broken, leafless tree branch to use in your Halloween decor? A glossy black or deep purple can be eerily spooky. The supplies can be found right outside your doorstep, making it an easy and budget-friendly project. Use smaller branches for tabletop decor and massive branches for your outdoor scary-scape.

Sunday Dinner Menu

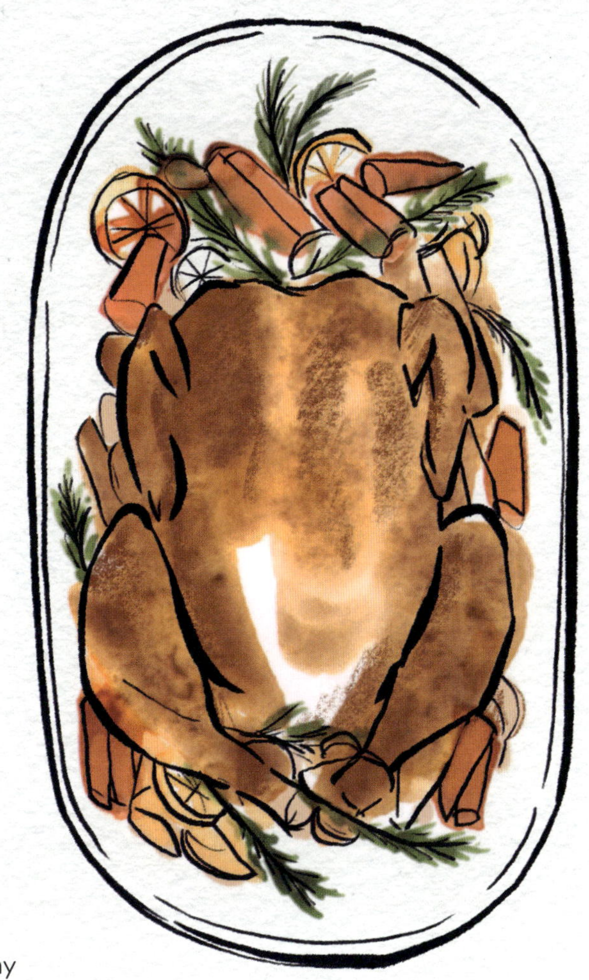

Who doesn't like pasta? *The answer was practically no one,* Rachael thought to herself. Even her picky-eater children liked pasta. Consequently, she could always whip up a batch of Ina Garten's arrabbiata red sauce. She made it so many times, she no longer had to consult the recipe. Whether for her family or unexpected guests, she could whip it up quickly, or better yet, pull a large batch out of the freezer. She knew to always have her larder stocked with the ingredients. It had saved her many times when she was tired, grumpy, and in no mood to cook—but still needed to get a healthy meal on the table. As Martha would say, having this kind of recipe in your back pocket is a "good thing." Made even better if you have a baguette in the freezer to unthaw and fresh greens in the garden for a table salad: fine dining any day of the week.

Back Pocket Cooking

WHY NOT TRY having one good Sunday dinner menu and recipe in your back pocket? Make sure you have the ingredients for it at all times in your larder, so that at any time, you have a recipe to make friends and family worthy of such status.

The Thrift Store Find

It was easily the most impressive, least-expensive living centerpiece she had ever displayed on her outdoor dining table. And it cost virtually nothing. It was on a shelf in the garage—a thrift store find—a tall, heavy, black metal candle holder with a pronounced spike in the center to stabilize a pillar candle. But she had other plans for it. A perfectly aged metal hanging basket sans the chain hanger was the perfect size and scale to perch on top of the candle holder, well secured and held in place by the jutting spike. She dropped in a lush vining geranium that spilled out over the sides, then placed it center stage on the table. The basket, elevated in such a way, was dramatic, with presence, especially when placed between two very tall thin iron taper candlesticks. Impressive. She loved the effect, and its ease of execution. *What else could she elevate in such an effortless way,* she thought? Anything her heart desired.

Raise It Up

WHY NOT TRY using pillar candlesticks as pedestals for . . . well, anything? Try potted plants, fresh fruit finials, or a plate for an instant cake stand. Use your imagination.

The Southwest Is Calling

It was a real paradigm shift. Learning a different language of beauty is part of the process of moving from the lushness and tall trees of Indiana or Tennessee to the parched, rustic grandeur of the Southwest. Yes, Colorado and Oklahoma and New Mexico had a much different way of communicating the beauty and magnificence of nature, in big and small ways, of course. If she wanted to remember those heady days of being young, and experiencing places like Santa Fe, New Mexico, and Durango, Colorado, for the first time, all she needed to do was burn some pinon wood. It was scented geography, and she adored it. Warm and nutty with overtones of spice and resin; if its scent were a color, it would be a dusty amber, evoking sunbaked earth and rocky foothills, open skies, and a landscape shaped by time and climate. Yes, it had become one of the scents of . . . home. Her home and her land. It was a personal thing. A scented mantra.

The Scented Pinion

WHY NOT TRY building a pinon fire or burning some pinon incense to capture the iconic smell of the Southwest? Woodsy, nutty, fresh, and piney, it's a singular, special fragrance to experience.

Joni Mitchell Told Me To

Billie had a certain look she was going for in her table setting. She was throwing a dinner party for a close friend and wanted to capture just the right mood of subtle sophistication. But all of her table linens seemed too brash and bright and strident. One in particular would work if it just was toned down by about 75 percent, she thought. Then it occurred to her: look at its underside and see if that would capture the vibe—hit just the right note of subtle moodiness she wanted to create. With strains of Joni Mitchell singing in her head to look at both sides now, she did just that. The wrong side of the linen cloth proved to be just the right side for her dinner table. Indeed, she would have to look at all of her tablecloths from both sides now.

From Both Sides Now

WHY NOT TRY using a tablecloth with the wrong side up for a different look? The reverse side might be equally as lovely, but in a different and softer tonal or textural way.

Be Ready to Make New Friends

Heidi loved everything about her new neighborhood. She loved the slam of the screen door at her favorite deli. She loved the thrift stores filled with fabulous finds; she loved the way everyone seemed to have a dog at their side walking through the town square, and how receptive local merchants were to their canine visitors. Not only was a doggy bowl with water provided for their refreshment, but most of them also had a small cache of doggy treats at the ready for any hungry pooch. What a small, but hospitable and humane expression of customer service. As soon as Heidi returned, she did the same at her own home. She unearthed a beautiful pottery urn with a lid and filled it with doggy treats to keep by the front door. So many neighbors had dogs that walked on the sidewalks in her neighborhood . . . it would be a special thing to give a treat to the sweet pets as they walked by. Plus, it was a good way to meet her new neighbors, and her neighbors' best friends.

Such a Good Doggy

WHY NOT TRY filling an interesting ornamental container with doggie treats to keep by your front door? It's a wonderful icebreaker to make new friends, both canine and human.

Melting Ghosts

Milkmen used to deliver milk to the door . . . now the Amazon or UPS delivery trucks deposit almost anything on your front porch. In anticipation of all of the holidays, especially Halloween around the corner, Monica had ordered a large box of tall white taper candles. As she pulled up in front of her home, she noticed them sitting on her front porch, exposed to a very warm and sunny October day. She hurriedly whisked them inside to get them out of the heat, fearing they would have melted into one solid mass. When she opened the box, indeed, some of the top ones were soft and misshapen. Immediately she tried to straighten the pliable wax, but in the process noticed how the bended forms, especially when further bent to the point of exaggeration, looked remarkably like hovering white ghost forms. Each of the candles depicted a different shadowy character. Monique immediately quit straightening them, instead twisting and bending them into a charming family of ethereal wax figures. She might even take it one step further and pull out a black marker to indicate eyes and make them look even more ghostlike in the black candlesticks she had on the mantle; they would look fabulous for her Halloween guests. As always, she had learned, sometimes it's not best to get overly distraught about something . . . before considering possible, sometimes very amusing, outcomes.

Wax Creations

WHY NOT TRY bending softened white taper candles into ghostly shapes? Create different ghostly personalities based on their size and shape. A whole family of ghosts is fun and fanciful.

Waste Not, Want Not in Your Kitchen

It really, really bothered Caleb. He wasted so much fresh produce from his own garden, the farmer's market, and his local grocer—even veggies gifted to him by neighbors. Still, he couldn't consume all of it easily and while still fresh. Then his sister, Elizabetta, shared a weekly habit she'd started in her own kitchen to prevent just such waste and unnecessary expense. "Before your fresh veggies and greens go south," she instructed, "go ahead and at the very least, **clean them and freeze them** if you don't have the time to actually **consume** them." She did it once a week while watching one of her favorite cooking shows. She said she found it relaxing and very gratifying to dice sweet and hot peppers, slice squash, and chiffonade chards and kales. Sometimes she'd even sauté them and freeze them in that state. Caleb especially hated when his basil went to waste, knowing how precious it was to him in the dead of winter. His food processor and olive oil solved that problem. Caleb hated to, once again, admit his older sibling was right, but indeed she was. A little effort, some disciplined and habitual effort, could solve his kitchen dilemma. Like Nike and Elizabetta say, "Just Do It!"

Don't Discard

WHY NOT TRY cleaning and freezing veggie remnants in bulk to use in soups and stews? Don't throw away what still has flavor. You can always make vegetable broth.

Child Prodigy

It was the cutest, dearest thing Birdie had ever seen. Her godson Goeffrey **loved** to draw, paint, and do all manner of things artistic. Even at the age of five he clearly had a gift, and Goeffrey's parents had his artwork displayed on almost every surface in their home. They were clearly proud of his talent, and their pride in him made Goeffrey that much more interested in it and improving his skill, though it is hard to improve on the innocent, primal beauty of a child's artistry. And that was what made this particular project so powerful. His mom took a piece of his art—a large baby zebra and its mama, to be exact—transferred it to a rug-sized canvas, and then needlepointed the rendering to create an original work of art in the form of a rug for his bedroom. It was perfect for the room's theme, as it was all about Goeffrey's fixation on wild animals from Africa. Stuffed lions and elephants and other animal toys were everywhere. Now this fabulous work of art, a family treasure, could join them.

Invaluable Art

WHY NOT TRY imprinting a child's artwork onto a blank needlepoint, pillow, ornament, or even a rug? It is guaranteed to be a masterpiece and raise the self-esteem of the artist.

Award-Winning Chocolate Chip Cookies

If you think it is just the dark chocolate chips in her cookies that make them special, you would be sorely mistaken. Deb had discovered the secret to award-winning chocolate chip cookies. She did indeed take first place for them at the state fair. And her secret was far from . . . secret. She told everyone that the key to their deliciousness was the tasty, pyramidal, delicate flakes of Maldon salt. Sprinkled on top just before or after baking, they took the goodies over the top, she preached. Since sharing the salty suggestion, Ida started using it on everything to elevate its yumminess. Avocado toast, grilled veggies, her own famous toffee. The salt could simply do no wrong. The key to chocolate chip cookie perfection . . . oh, and all those pecans she puts in . . .

Salty Goodness

WHY NOT TRY using the unique pyramid flakes of Maldon salt to enhance flavors in both sweet and savory dishes? It also makes a great gift.

Johnny Gets a Cooking Lesson

Finally, it had gotten cool enough to make their first batch of chicken and dumplings for the fall season. Their family always made it an occasion to be noted; ritualized in a way. Now, it was time for the passing of the culinary torch, so to speak, and Johnny was getting a cooking lesson on making one of their favorite family meals. "The intense deliciousness," Mom said, "was all about depth of flavor. And the depth of flavor comes from the fond." She stated this in a way that communicated magic and secrets. She showed her son how to brown the chicken just so. Be patient and don't crowd the pan. That's the key. They looked together at the valuable golden-brown bits of chicken stuck to the bottom of the pan. "That," she said, "is the stuff of magic." She went on to describe browning other meats and veggies with the same transformative mystical power. The alchemy was complete, when with a flourish, she added some dry sherry and broth to deglaze the pan, and a cloud of steamy fragrance erupted over the stove. Fond = cooking magic.

Browned Bits

WHY NOT TRY optimizing and learning about the power of the fond in your cooking? The fond is the culinary term for the caramelized bits of food that are left on the bottom of a pan after cooking.

Easy and Delicious Protein-Packed Food

Skeeter was trying to increase the amount of protein she consumed. Her doctor and nutritionist both told her that a sad fact of aging is that we begin to lose muscle mass. Consequently, exercise and protein intake became essential to aging well, staying fit, and being able to continue enjoying the high energy sports she loved, like tennis and skiing. She wasn't a big fan of eating meat and had to do a bit of research on high protein foods from other sources. And one of them was a perfect example of what she wanted being what she needed. She never considered the nutritional value of edamame when she frequently ate at the Japanese restaurant around the corner—always ordering the delicious pods as an appetizer. When she learned that a cup of it carried a walloping 13 grams of protein, she started to eat it in other ways at home, not just dining out. She added it to her salads, rice bowls, soups, and stews. She'd add it to her breakfast cereal if she could, she loved it that much. Edamame was packed with protein, so now her freezer was packed with it. Good logical nutrition.

Nutritional Pods

WHY NOT TRY eating edamame in a variety of ways to increase your protein intake?

School Supplies Aren't Just for Kids

It was basic math to Mina. School supplies = September, no matter how old the student. Long after Mina's kids had graduated and moved out, she still couldn't resist the allure of school supplies, the scent of #2 pencils, and the excitement of a new lunchbox. When buying groceries or toilet paper at the superstore, she couldn't resist checking out the school supply aisles and their offerings of highlighters, pencil cases, and notebooks. Especially the notebooks. And all on sale for ridiculously low prices with the start of school around the corner—"loss leaders" that retailers used to entice customers in to buy other merchandise at full price. Well, she took the bait. She may not be about to start fourth grade, but she could still use some fresh composition notebooks (her favorites), a few glue sticks for crafts, and a supply of her favorite fine-tip pens. *After all, why should kids have all the fun?* she asked herself as she filled her basket and took a whiff of those yellow pencils.

Adult School Supplies

WHY NOT TRY purchasing your **own** school supplies when they're on sale in the fall?

Grab the Dye!

Durn! Leah had spilled coffee on her favorite white sun dress, and for some reason stain remover and detergent weren't taking out the stain. The coffee dribbles were a mocha color she actually liked, but not on her favorite piece of clothing. While rummaging through her laundry room cabinet for bleach or more powerful stain remover, Leah came across a box of fabric dye she'd used last year for a tie-dyeing project—napkins, to be exact. She loved the way they turned out, and loved the color, an earthy coffee brown. She'd had enough with the stain removal drama. Now she had bigger plans for the dress. Wouldn't it look lovely in this brown shade that would perfectly camouflage the stain? Problem solved and a new favorite dress in the works. And in the color of the coming season—cafe latte!

Transformation

WHY NOT TRY hiding a coffee stain on a favorite blouse or dress with fabric dye instead of discarding it?

A Closet Full of Clothes with Nothing to Wear

Leisl couldn't figure it out. She had a closet full of clothes she liked, but still felt she had nothing to wear most of the time, or clothes she **liked** to wear and felt were becoming and flattering. She decided at the new year when cleaning out her closet that she needed to be more methodical about it. She would do a little research to make dressing easier in the morning and her wardrobe more cost effective. YouTube to the rescue, when the library (her preferred resource on such things) came up short. In went her search terms: short waisted, long legged, short neck, few curves, and so on. Out came video recommendations addressing all of her issues, with some very specific suggestions: opt for V necks versus crew neck blouses and sweaters; vertical versus horizontal stripes; and avoid overly wide belts and defined waistlines.

A closet inventory was warranted. She tried on versions of the various recommendations, and also pieces and shapes to avoid. Well, I'll be durned. They were spot on. *I should have watched those videos years ago*, she said to herself, as her stack of crew neck sweaters to give away grew and grew. YouTube for the win! In Leisl's closet at least.

Targeted Wardrobe Tips

WHY NOT TRY gathering fashion tips from YouTube and other sources? You can make yourself look taller, or thinner, or older or younger, or long-waisted or . . . well, whatever the style issue you want to address.

Hidden Alley Garden

Jules had a problem. Too many seeds, and too little real estate to garden in. Even though she had a beautiful, somewhat expansive garden, it wasn't as large as the garden she had left behind. She missed having the space for annual bloomers like poppies and hollyhocks, celosia and Queen Anne's lace: flowers that went to seed abundantly, bloomed their heads off, then usually succumbed to spider mites or the intense heat of summer. She was thinking this as she took the trash out to the bins in her alley. Then inspiration struck. It might not be front and center for all to see, but there was a patch of bare earth running parallel to the alley behind her home along the fence line—a forgotten and uncultivated area, but a space with great gardening potential. Before she knew it, she was on her hands and knees, weeding, and removing whatever scruffy green was growing there. She roughed up the soil, not really caring how fertile it was or wasn't, then sprinkled some of her extra hollyhock seeds in the troughs she made. As added insurance in case the hollyhocks were not happy, she also sprinkled some excess larkspur seed that was about to expire. She then covered the seeds, gave them a bit of a sprinkle, and walked away, brushing the dirt from her hands. *They may or may not germinate,* she thought, *but what a wonderful opportunity to take a tiny garden risk with some marginally viable seeds, and in an otherwise forgotten space.* What a happy surprise it would be for the kids coming home from school when they took a shortcut through the alley.

Secret Gardens

WHY NOT TRY gardening in forgotten places like neglected or out of sight areas? Try an alley, or a muddy, blank area near the garage or on the side of the house. What's there to lose? There is a low risk and high reward.

Iris or Cornstalks or Both?

There were two types of plants that had gone wild along the sidewalk-side fence line in her neighborhood—some kind of wild perennial geranium with a maroon-colored flower and banks of old-fashioned iris in antique hues of lavender and tawny gold. Both seemed to like the crowded conditions between the brick wall and the fences and had responded accordingly with great vigor. As she was walking in the old neighborhood, looking at Halloween decor and pumpkin displays, she noticed how closely the dried detached leaves of the iris looked like the foliage of corn stalks and corn husks used at that time of year in autumnal arrangements. She gathered a large bunch of the leaves whose form and texture seemed just right and took them home where she lovingly made a bed of the leaves for her ornamental pumpkins. She loved the result, thinking the still life arrangements on her front steps now looked far more natural and "finished." Pleased and feeling quite smug, she went inside to make a cup of pumpkin-spice tea to enjoy while sitting on the front porch and admiring her handiwork.

Looks Like . . .

WHY NOT TRY using the dry, spear-shaped leaves of iris foliage to mimic dried corn stalks in your fall arrangements? If you can't access dried corn stalks yet still crave something seasonal for your autumn decor, the dried leaves of iris are thick, buttery colored, and tough, not unlike that of corn, and they make a fine, more urban-available alternative for arrangements, indoors and out.

An Old Pumpkin Fills the Space

What to do, what to do? Clarice wanted to get these last massive containers potted up before the day's end. Two large and stately boxwood cones were ready and waiting to frame the formal entry leading to the front door. But she had underestimated the amount of potting soil she would need and knew she would come up short. She glanced up at the voracious squirrels, destroying and nibbling each of the mass of pumpkins on the steps. Pumpkin carcass carnage and pumpkin seeds were everywhere. *That's it,* she squealed to herself. A two for one solution. She picked up a couple of the larger half-chewed pumpkins and plopped them into one of the huge pots. Then she did the same in the other pot. Now she would have more than enough potting soil to plant both of them—seeing as the pumpkins took up so much space. They would compost in place, nicely feeding the shrubs . . . she was cleaning up a big old mess . . . they wouldn't end up in the trash bin . . . they were saving money on potting soil . . . and she didn't have to go to her local nursery and would be done by day's end. Problem, meet pumpkin solution.

A Squashy Solution

WHY NOT TRY using a rotting pumpkin after Halloween to fill up space in a large container planting? It saves on soil and keeps the pumpkin out of the landfill.

In the Eye of the Beholder

It was the interesting, textural shadows Polly noticed first. The pale brick wall made a wonderful movie screen for the waving forms of the tall grassy seed heads in the alley. The strappy green foliage and tawny, spiky seed heads were stunning, even if they were considered weeds. Arching Indian grass skullcaps looked like feathers, and quivering quake oat grass almost seemed to glow in the late summer sun. On a whim, she cut several stems, and after checking for buggy hitchhikers, brought them inside to fill a glass jelly jar in the windowsill. A few golden Rudbeckia from her perennial garden gave the arrangement a very specific prairie charm. She could picture pioneer women doing the same, placing the rustic combo on an old wood table to provide a bit of simple, earthy cheer. Even better, it didn't cost a cent. She sighed with contentment, then proceeded to make an early dinner for herself. A bowl of stew somehow seemed appropriate.

Who Would Have Thought?

WHY NOT TRY making a bouquet with weeds? Just be mindful of those that cause allergies or skin sensitivities!

Garden Gifts

Linny's mother loved the thick glossy leaves of the iconic magnolias of the South. She grew to love them when they lived for a time in Knoxville, Tennessee. She missed them, along with the vibrant red berry clusters of the many nandina and winterberry plantings in her old garden. Her deep affection for both persisted after moving north again to her Indiana home. All geographies and zones have their unique treasures. Her mother's birthday was on November 30, and in an Aha! moment while gardening at her own Southern home, Linny came up with a brilliant idea. She grabbed some sharp hand pruners and proceeded to cut branch after branch off the Southern magnolia growing in her front yard. She wrapped the ends in damp paper towels and arranged them in a large cardboard box. She placed a dry cleaner bag over this layer and then created a second layer of clusters of vibrant nandina berries. She imagined the look on her mom's face when she opened the box, and delighted in the ways she knew she would use them. *Gifts from the garden are always the best*, she thought as she taped up the box to send North.

Geographical Gifting

WHY NOT TRY mailing magnolia leaves and berries to someone who lives in the North, if you live in the South? The recipients might miss them from a former home or want to experience them at the holidays for the first time.

Be Prepared for Special Surprises

It was a delightful idea—keeping a "kit" in your car to meet the moment when an interesting seed head, bank of sunflowers, bark, branches, pinecones, or another of nature's treasures presented themselves. The idea was not hers, but the mother of a school chum who was an artist, a naturalist, a science teacher . . . and most importantly, someone who had an eye for beauty. In areas that were deemed appropriate—on private land with permission (no state or national parks)—she could find all sorts of treasures and surprises. The experience was made all the better because she was prepared with her kit of sharpened secateurs and scissors, plastic bags, and seed envelopes. On occasion, she would bring even a bucket of water and a tarp to bundle up large branches or arching grasses. What treasures are literally at our feet and within arm's length if we take the time to observe nature's gifts. It made her feel resourceful. A real pioneer woman, using the bounty of the earth.

Be Prepared

WHY NOT TRY making a foraging kit to keep in your car? Add pruners, baggies, a pocketknife, seed envelopes, and garden gloves.

Round Peg in a Square Hole

A landscaper friend of hers shared this most brilliant, intuitive, but still unusual planting practice: digging a square hole for planting a large shrub or tree rather than the traditional round hole. She'd had her share of experiences with girdled tree roots and circling root systems that couldn't seem to break free from their container-grown pattern to penetrate the clay soil of their new in-ground environment. Round and round those roots grew in their round hole, eventually almost strangling the plant in the process. Ah! But a square hole would help defy this pattern and allow those roots to expand, eventually making their way into the square and then beyond. Out instead of around, liberated and happy! A round peg in a square hole, so to speak.

Be Square

WHY NOT TRY digging a square hole for trees and shrubs instead of a round hole? This prevents root girdling and helps the plant establish more quickly and successfully.

Treasure Hunt in the Garden

When Camellia was in high school, she delighted in foraging lush plants in the woods behind her childhood home. She dug up tiny upstart trees and various miniature ferns and planted them in pots to bring indoors to her growing houseplant collection. They delighted her—lush and green and free for the taking, no less. Many years later, while working in her own garden with her two boys, Camellia remembered the delightful practice and sent her boys out on a hunt for their own tiny volunteers of spruce, laurel, and redbuds in the woods at the back of their property. They especially loved the glossy green starts of hellebores that had seeded themselves everywhere. Carefully potting them up in tiny clay terracotta pots with instructions on minding their tender roots was as much fun as the hunt, and the project proved to be a wonderful, nostalgic, and hands-on way to spend a beautiful spring morning. Shopping their own property for plants—a very special treasure hunt indeed.

Shop Your Garden

WHY NOT TRY shopping your garden for potted plants, topiaries, and ornamentals? Volunteer trees, shrubs, and flowers are everywhere in your landscape. Shop your garden first.

Gathering of Family and Foliage

Of course, one could be conventional and have a florist do their dinner party centerpiece. But Jackie wasn't a conventional kind of gal and wanted something unconventional and extremely seasonal to decorate her tables. She was considering different options on her walk through her neighborhood, the streets lined with magnificent sycamore trees. Mounds of their mammoth leaves scattered the sidewalk in shades of mahogany, walnut, and brown butter. She started gathering them, stem by stem, shade by shade, into a hand bouquet—a leaf bouquet. The result was marvelous. Tone on tone, almost mimicking rich shades of wood. Some positioned one direction, others in another. The long stems made the composition easy and effortless. *What if,* she thought, *I secured the stems with some transparent little rubber bands . . . and then ran them in multiples up and down the long table?* She could add height to them, but not enough to obscure the vision of guests talking across the table, by placing them on her tall spiral brass candlesticks. Before she even got home, Jackie had a plan, and a spectacular centerpiece, in mind.

Leafy Loveliness

WHY NOT TRY making fall leaf bouquets with long-stemmed fall foliage? Use all one variety or mix up colors and leaf shapes.

Einstein and Centerpieces

Gorgeous lemons with lemon foliage tucked in seem to be everywhere these days, Lila noticed. Every furniture catalog and Pinterest image showcasing a large island or beautiful dining table seemed to use it as a focal point. No wonder, as its elegant and natural simplicity renders the arrangement sheer perfection. She realized every Nancy Meyers movie, with their lust-worthy interiorscapes, uses the same simple formula: a beautiful container, be it a basket, bowl, or cake stand, plus a singular seasonal fruit and foliage that is evocative of that fruit in its natural growing state. Its uncomplicated organic beauty makes it the essence of elegant simplicity. It was like that quotation attributed to Albert Einstein: "Make everything as simple as possible, but no simpler." Lila needed look no further for centerpiece inspiration for her dinner party that night. Thanks, Al.

Elegant Simplicity

WHY NOT TRY using a large bowl filled with one type of fruit or fresh cut greenery as a simple and seasonal centerpiece?

Comfy-Chic Weekend Attire

Sonya loved wearing her adult sons' oversized flannel shirts and button-downs as part of her weekend wardrobe. Tres comfortable, and in a funny way, it made her miss them less. If pressed and worn over some flattering leggings with dainty ballet flats, the combo looked comfy **and** chic. Both effortless and stylish simultaneously. *Very Audrey Hepburn*, Sonia thought as she hugged herself from a chilly autumn breeze. She may have to look through their stored clothing again. Maybe there were some oversized comfy sweaters she could add to her wardrobe as well.

Raid His Closet

WHY NOT TRY raiding your son's or husband's closet for oversized dress shirts to wear with leggings and ballet flats for a comfortable chic look?

Gingham, Let Me Introduce You to Plaid and Leopard

Annie was a play-by-the-rules kind of girl, at school, at home, and at work. But she also had a creative streak that refused to be ignored and was crying to express itself . . . even at the tender age of eleven. She especially liked to dress with flair and originality, but wearing a uniform to school suppressed her appetite for more daring combinations, more than just school-girl plaid with white and navy. Entering junior high next year would release her from uniforms and unleash her joy of color, pattern, and scale. Out would come her plaid skirts paired with similarly colored tiny, flowered ginghams. Unexpected combinations compared to her peers, but wearing them made her feel special and unexpected herself. And she liked that feeling. Who's to say no? Maybe she was a bit of a rule breaker after all. Daring tights, bold colors, unique shoes, hats, and socks. Mixing it up and playing with uncommon and unexpected combinations gave her confidence and flair, and helped her develop her sense of composition and perspective. It was liberating and fun.

Coordinate Your Prints

WHY NOT TRY getting out of your fashion comfort zone? Layer plaid sweaters with floral prints or animal prints with stripes. Look for color echoes and the scale of the print to determine good wardrobe companions.

Open the Champagne for a Closet Consultation

Penelope wanted to have her own stylist. It wasn't that she needed one—she was quite capable of putting together both classy and casual outfits. Still, she wanted a fresh take on her pieces, both clothing and accessories, and she knew she had **more** than enough to work with. Pieces she loved but didn't wear, both new and old. As she was sifting through a bunch of recent photos, she came up with a brilliant idea, if she did say so herself. Penelope was quite fortunate to have more than one stylish niece in their twenties and thirties who had great youthful, but classic style. Maybe she could entice them with champagne, good music, and the possibility of lots of girlish fun? They could play dress up in her closet, just like they did when they were small, but this time with an objective. Help Aunt Penelope put together new outfits and clothing combos to make better and more creative use of what she had. It would be a great time—a really fun time—if she could coordinate all of their schedules to make it happen. Before the idea escaped her, she picked up her phone to text the two of them, making it sound as fun and rewarding as possible. These were girls who knew their way around fashion . . . and good hand-me-downs.

A New Point of View

WHY NOT TRY letting someone younger or older than you come up with new fresh wardrobe combinations for you? A different eye creates different layers and styles.

Size Matters

Terri was seeing a pattern—a quite cute one at that. She was traveling in Europe and began to notice something: how much smaller things were over there than in the States. The default on almost everything in the States, from cars to portion sizes, was that bigger was better—and not just in Texas. But in this part of the world, smaller seemed to be valued more. Small cars, smaller bottles and jars of things in the grocery store, smaller servings in restaurants. When she returned home, she found it charming and smart (she was space and storage challenged in her apartment) to look for smaller and more compact versions of all sorts of things: the tiny zucchinis and cucumbers at the grocery store, smaller cans of soda pop, and tiny pots of succulents at the nursery. She really took it to heart. Did she **really** need a huge jar of mayo, or would the smaller size be sufficient? She observed that, yes, there was a great big world out there to discover, and a lovely small world as well.

Dollhouse Living

WHY NOT TRY thinking small and looking for small, dwarf varieties of vegetables and fruits at the grocery store or shrubs at the nursery? Do you really need to keep buying that supersize jar of mayonnaise, or will the smaller version do?

By the Fire

Okay, maybe it was still a balmy 79°F (26°C) out, but Stella wasn't going to miss the annual first fire of the season at her local bookstore. She loved these kinds of traditions. You would think that the last Saturday in October would be cool enough to accommodate the yearly tradition, but when it came to the weather, all bets were off. Still, people were laughing, book browsing, drinking free hot chocolate with cookies, and having a lovely time. She had yet to light her first wood fire of the season at her home and was looking forward to the coziness of it all. *Maybe I should start making it an annual fete with my family to honor the changing of the seasons, and the arrival of cold weather?* she thought to herself. Her kids would love it; like most children, they loved any reason to celebrate. Couple it with her first batch of their favorite chicken and dumplings recipe and you had the makings of something special. Traditions were about consistency and a sense of security and love, after all. *Something you can count on—unlike the weather,* she chuckled to herself. Maybe even some warm apple or pumpkin pie, the first of fall, could be celebrated right along with those chicken and dumplings.

Ceremonial Firsts

WHY NOT TRY making an occasion out of the first fire of fall? Indoors or out, serve a favorite soup or stew and mark it as an annual event and a favorite home ritual.

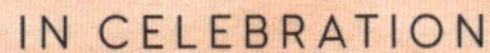

Flowers by the Can

It was Edna's first experience serving on a fundraiser committee for her child's elementary school class. This year, the fundraiser featured an Italian dinner, and her responsibility was to provide the centerpieces. She was informed that there would be as many as twenty tables, and the more money they could save on supplies, the larger their profit margin would be. Edna tapped into her creative reservoirs and recalled a family reunion that might hold the solution. For one of the reunion dinners, they canvased local Italian restaurants and requested their empty commercial cans of tomatoes and other veggies, which were then repurposed as large vases for each table. These vases were filled with cut zinnias, branches of edible peppers, branches of herbs, and other abundant summer blooms. Empty wine bottles were used as candleholders, with the only expense being the candles themselves. They bought some of the old-fashioned candles that dripped in multiple colors—think Chianti bottles. Voila! An idea she could easily replicate for the fundraiser dinner. Satisfied that she had found a solution, she began making a list of Italian restaurants and pizza parlors in her area.

Centerpiece in a Can

WHY NOT TRY using large produce cans with interesting labels as table vases for large gatherings? They're inexpensive, dramatic, and colorful.

Memories and Friendship in Bloom

Maggie's friend Robin had just lost her dad and was devastated. They were both gardeners and flower lovers. Instinctively, Maggie started thinking about flowers to send and then caught herself. When Maggie's brother died, she remembered how depressing it had been to have all of those dying bouquets and sympathy notes around the house, wilting, sour-smelling, and having to be disposed of. Maggie had a better idea. It was November—bulb-planting time in their garden zone. She wrote a note to her friend and told her that she had 200 daffodil bulbs (Robin's dad's favorite flower) to plant in the field behind Robin's home. They could plant them together, drink some wine, and share stories about Robin's dad. It would be good for both of them. Most importantly, when the daffodils bloom next spring, it will be such a lovely memory of Robin's dad and their friendship for many years to come.

Field of Memories

WHY NOT TRY planting spring bulbs for a friend when their loved one passes? It will give them something to enjoy next season and to remember their loved one by—certainly more enduring than sending cut flowers.

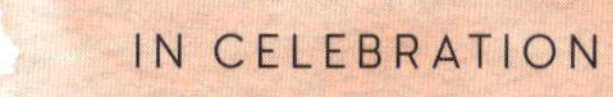

The Good Neighbor

He could tell from the tall grass and the unedged turf that the widower T.R. next door was feeling low, maybe even sick, as he hadn't seen T.R. out feeding the birds the last two mornings. T.R. had been picking up his paper each day, (he was old school and still had it delivered) so he knew T.R. wasn't away visiting his kids. All of this rumination took place as he was stirring a huge pot of chicken, chili, and rice soup, far more than he and his wife and son could consume in the course of a meal. So, he spooned a generous portion into a glass jar after it cooled, cut and wrapped a large wedge of cornbread from the old cast-iron skillet, and grabbed one of the ripe teeny-tiny avocados from a bag he had just brought home. Sliced on top of the chili, it was divine, especially with a squirt of lime juice. He knew this from experience. He grabbed a lime, assembled it all neatly, and declared it a "random act of dinner" for his friend T.R.. *It was a twofer,* he thought. T.R. would surely appreciate a home-cooked meal, and it gave him a good excuse to check in on him without seeming like a "helicopter" neighbor. T.R. was an independent guy with gumption and resolve. He'd be fine in the long run. In the meantime, a little comfort food could do no harm. Knowing T.R., he would probably want the recipe.

Random Act of Dinner

WHY NOT TRY a "random act of dinner"? Whether it's a lack of time, a lack of will, or a lack of culinary skill, we all seem to be lacking that comfort of all comforts, a good ol' home-cooked meal. Next time you are doing some batch cooking, prepare an extra meal to-go for someone who really needs it.

"Everything Is Copy"

Her son Johnny did it, even before hearing the quote from Nora Ephron that "Everything is copy." Everything . . . and everyone. Johnny was a writer and always watching, observing, and listening to the people in his life; coworkers, customers at his favorite coffee shop, his doctor, and the custodian in his building. "They were," he told his mother, "all potential characters in a book or story." Of course, when watching movies or reading a book, it is those characters (with all their eccentricities and irritations) that are often the most compelling. He told her that it had significantly improved the quality and richness of his days when he started looking at the people in his life that way. *Wow,* his mother thought. *He's absolutely spot on.* Not only that, the next time she got irritated with the overly chatty lady behind the drugstore counter, she would remember . . . and maybe be a bit more patient and attentive in the process.

Your Life Is a Story

WHY NOT TRY looking at your life and the people in it as characters in a book? Quirky, kind, gifted, annoying—doing so makes the course of a day far more interesting and might even help us be more tolerant and patient. Let the story of your life and the characters in it unfold.

With Age Comes Wisdom and Common Sense

It was a secret of adulthood, Gretchen Rubin, the writer, would say, learned from years of looking for misplaced or hidden things. Whether it's a specific garden tool, your car keys, or a condiment in your fridge—whatever you are looking for is probably in the place you think it is, or the place you last used it. You just haven't looked hard enough, or thoroughly enough in that spot. Maybe you glanced into that box, but didn't look underneath the things stored on top of it. You looked in your purse for your keys, but didn't look well enough in each pocket of said purse. You felt sure your sunglasses were in the car, but didn't see them because they were wedged in the seat. The moral of this story: Take the time to be thorough and really intentional when looking for an item where you think it is. Even if you don't see it on the first pass, it's probably right in front of you, just hidden by your impatience while looking.

Secret of Adulthood

WHY NOT TRY being more intentional and thorough when looking for something you can't find? Hint: It's probably where you think it is.

Dad's So Smart

Her dad was the first person to tell her about the Zeigarnik effect—the theory that an activity is more readily recalled and resumed when it has been interrupted or left incomplete. He would use it to demonstrate tools for increased productivity and efficiency in the workplace. *Why not,* she thought, *try employing the technique in writing the next chapters of her book?* Here's how she could do it: each time she sat at her desk to write, she would complete one section. Instead of stopping there, she would begin writing one or two paragraphs of the next portion—leaving it glaringly incomplete. She knew that the nagging thought of the unfinished idea would beckon her back to the page, ready and waiting for completion. In a good, creative way, it would wake her in the middle of the night, or early in the morning, completing the concept. She knew when she sat back at her desk, the work would already have been written in her head. Now it was just putting the words on the page. Thanks, Dad.

Psychological Motivator

WHY NOT TRY using the Zeigarnik effect? This work of Lithuanian-Soviet psychologist, Bluma Zeigarnik, and her colleague Maria Ovsiankina, can help you to stay motivated and on task when working on a project.

College Midterm Stress

There she was, collecting one after another, sometimes handfuls, of the papery tan seed heads. Maple seed "helicopters," they called them, because of their graceful rotating motion when falling to the ground—like the rotary blades of a helicopter. Fascinating and soothing to watch. So much so, her friend told her, that she collects bagfuls of them for her young niece in college. They made great stress relievers for her and her friends during midterms and finals. How very clever, whimsical, and ingenious. And a great low-cal, inexpensive alternative to midnight pizza.

Twirling Stress Release

WHY NOT TRY using maple seed helicopters as stress relievers? Watching them gracefully twirl in the wind reduces tension and helps calm anxious thoughts. They also make great alternatives to throwing rice at a wedding.

Make a Plan

"We need to get it done," Jini told Elizabeth, "but somehow we just keep putting it off." Elizabeth had the same problem. Jini and her husband, and Elizabeth and hers, needed to execute their living wills, properly drafted, signed, and safely and securely accessible for their kids to reference, just in case—advance care planning. The four of them were all best friends and, along with their kids, needed to know what to do if they were seriously ill and couldn't communicate their wishes about medical care. They needed to get their wishes in writing in a living will, a type of advance directive that would name a proxy who would have power to make decisions on their behalf. The two of them decided to take the bull by the horns and make the onerous task a little more enticing. They began to plan a dinner party for the four of them and their three adult children to discuss their end-of-life preferences . . . before it got too depressing to discuss. As they understood it, they could download free forms from their state, complete them, and then witness and notarize each other's documents. One of their neighbors was a notary, and wouldn't mind notarizing the papers, she was sure. Once they had them drafted appropriately, and shared with everyone where the documents were stored . . . they all could check one great big old important thing off their list of things they **had** to do.

Let's Do It Together

WHY NOT TRY making an event out of signing or witnessing important documents to ensure it actually gets done?

What Are Friends For?

Fiona couldn't get out of the bathtub. She'd torn a disc in her back, though she didn't know it at the time, and her husband, out of town on business, wasn't available to help her. Fortunately, she had her cellphone nearby and was able to call her bestie to help her escape from the now-cold bath. Neither of them had adult children or family members nearby and both had spouses that traveled frequently for their jobs. When they began to engage in various scenarios of imaginary horribles where being alone in such circumstances could be difficult or even dangerous, the two made a pact. On those occasions when either of them were "living solo," they needed to do a daily check in with one another to assure themselves all was well. A text would be fine, or a drop by visit, or, of course, a phone call. Just in case you happened to be in a pickle and couldn't get out of a jam . . . or a bathtub.

Let's Make a Pact

WHY NOT TRY making a pact with your friends to check on one another while "living solo," even if it's temporary?

CONCLUSION

Why Not Try . . .

- Seeing with eyes that take nothing for granted? Hearing with ears that truly listen? Speaking with empathy and clarity and confidence? Tasting what is original and irresistible? And touching the lives of others, both friends and strangers, with goodness and caring?
- Anything new, anything exciting—anything you want to learn? Experiencing places and people and things, both large and small, near and far, will nourish your senses and spirits.
- Finding contentment and creativity in the ordinary course of a day? For truly, no day is ordinary, just perhaps not fully mined for its potential. Truly it is the daily ritualistic little things that set the tone of our lives.

There are no small things if they give you joy.

INDEX

ABOUT THE AUTHOR

Linda is a self-taught garden designer and stylist who also writes and produces garden media for TV, magazines, Instagram, YouTube, and the web. She lived and gardened for over thirty years in her 1935 English Tudor home before moving to her very lively "Cottage on the Hill" in Oklahoma City. Her gardens have been featured in numerous national and local magazines and have been toured more times than she can count.

Linda looks at everything—her home, family, travel, and life's biggest questions—through a gardening lens. Gardening has helped her raise two boys, be a better friend and neighbor, learn resilience, and, at times, saved her sanity. She says often that gardening is simultaneously one of the most joyous and frustrating things she does. She is the author of *The Elegant and Edible Garden* and *The Garden Journal*, available online and in bookstores. Join Linda on this great adventure that is gardening.